Angling in the English Stream

Angling in the English Stream

100 Ordinary English Words:
Caught, Filleted, and Served Up in
Tasty Little Essays

By David Schelhaas

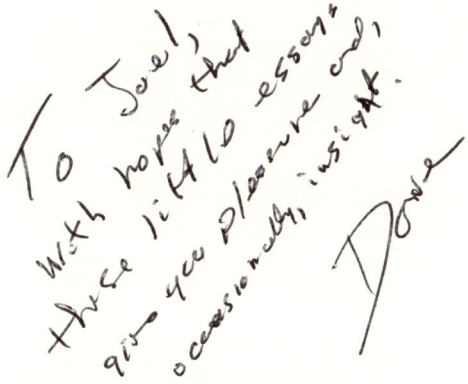

Dordt College Press, Sioux Center, Iowa

Copyright © 2003 by David Schelhaas

Fragmentary portions of this book may be freely used by those who are interested in furthering its appreciation of words and language, so long as the material is not pirated for monetary gain and so long as proper credit is visibly given to the publisher and the author. Others, and those who wish to use larger sections of text, must seek written permission from the publisher.

Printed in the United States of America.

Dordt College Press
498 Fourth Avenue NE
Sioux Center, Iowa 51250
United States of America
ISBN: 0-932914-53-5

www.dordt.edu/dordt_press

The Library of Congress Cataloging-in-Publication Data
is on file with the Library of Congress, Washington, D.C.

Library of Congress Control Number: 2003116485

For my wife Jeri—
whose words of good sense and vibrant love
have furnished all the rooms we've lived in.

Foreword

I am a fisherman—have been for just about as long as I can remember. My family did not take many vacations when I was a boy, but one day a week in the summer we would pack a picnic lunch in mid-afternoon and head for Lake Shetek where we'd pay a quarter to drive through a farmer's pasture and fish from his shore.

Fifty years later I still love to fish—from shore, from a boat, or through the ice. I'm not fanatical about it, and I don't buy all the latest gear. Even after fifty years, I'm not an especially good fisherman, but on a warm June day when the walleye are biting or a bright fall day when the perch are going crazy, I'd rather be fishing than doing anything else.

But, I am *not* an angler, that is, I've never called myself an angler. If I called up my brother and said, "You want to do a little angling today?" he might just hang up on me. In the part of Minnesota—land of 10,000 lakes—where I grew up, people don't call themselves anglers without getting funny looks.

Nevertheless, *angle* (*angler, angling*) was the word used by our linguistic ancestors, the English, to describe the act of fishing. Why? Because an *angle* was a hook, and fishing is the art of hooking fish. The very word *English* derives from that old word meaning "hook." The Angles who migrated to the place that was later called England (Angleland) came from an area on the Jutland peninsula that was shaped like a hook. Thus, from a hook-shaped land a people's name was derived, and from that name came the word to designate the most widely used language in the world today. (For a more thorough explanation, see the second essay in this book.)

I've called this little book *Angling in the English Stream* because what I try to do here is hook some English words, fillet them, and serve them up to you in ways that are tasty, succulent, and nourishing. Izaak Walton, that ancient English fisherman who wrote the first great treatise on fishing, called his book *The Compleat Angler*. This book is far from complete. The total catch is only one hundred of the more than 500,000 words (some say there may be as many as a million) in the English language. And no word is completely gutted or filleted.

The reason for the brevity is that these little word essays were first of all given on the radio, and the aural nature of radio usually requires simple words and brief explanations. The fact that I wrote these pieces to be spoken and heard has affected my style in other ways as well, as I'm sure you'll notice.

I began "What's the Good Word," the short radio spot I have had on KDCR radio in Sioux Center, Iowa, because of my own fascination with the stories in words and my conviction that most language users would find these stories as interesting as I do. So often in my years as an English teacher, students and others asked me to explain the connection between two similar words—or even homonyms. "What's the relationship between *rake* meaning the leaf-gathering, scraping tool, the *rake* that describes the slant to the floor of certain auditoriums, and the *rake* used to describe a dissolute man?" How can a native speaker not wonder about such things? Well, this little book answers those sorts of questions.

Henry Higgins in Shaw's *Pygmalion* says, "Remember that you are a human being with a soul and the divine gift of articulate speech: that your native language is the language of Shakespeare and Milton and the Bible, and don't sit their crooning like a bilious pigeon." His concern is with the sounds coming from the mouth of the flower girl Eliza Doolittle, but what he says can be applied to other aspects of the language as well.

The English language is as deep and fertile as an ocean and the gift of articulate speech, a divine gift; yet most of our school education focuses on just one aspect of that language, its grammar. Why shouldn't a girl who runs the hurdles in high school learn that those little portable fences that she jumps over connect her linguistically with British sheepherders of a thousand years ago? Why shouldn't we explain what *mess* means when we say that Esau sold his birthright for a mess of pottage? My hope for *Angling in the English Language* is that it will enhance the reader's sense of delight and wonder: delight in the hidden stories most words contain and wonder at the marvelous, erratic journeys most words have taken as they have been used across the centuries.

This book is intended for ordinary readers—not linguists, philologists, etymologists, or language historians. I come to the language as an amateur, an untrained lover of the language, one who has not studied its history or etymology in any formal way but only taught its literature for many years.

One of the great repositories of English words is the *King James Bible*. Since "What's the Good Word" ran on Dordt College radio, a Christian college radio station with a many Christian listeners, I often included references to King James word usages as well as those from other early Bible translations (Caxton's and Langland's especially). Because of the Christian audience, I also often included an observation related to living the Christian life. All the essays in this book make some sort of biblical connection, and some of them have the flavor of a meditation. But it would be inaccurate to call it a book of meditations; it's simply a book of word stories and reflections that touches directly or indirectly on things religious.

I would not recommend that anyone read it straight through, but then I don't know how it should be read. A few essays at a time? One a day? Weekends only while you're waiting for the fish to bite?

However you do it, good fishing to you.

Alas

Some time ago the hymnal of my church was revised. This process seems to occur every thirty years, so I remember the red hymnal, the blue one, and now, the gray one. This new gray hymnal has been criticized because certain old hymns have been eliminated but also because certain new hymns have been included. But most of the criticism has been aimed at the changes made in the language of familiar psalms and hymns that were kept in the hymnal. In an attempt to eliminate archaic diction and usage, the hymnal committee changed words and phrases of familiar hymns. I'm sure all of us who use the hymnal have had the experience of singing an old favorite lustily, from memory, with our heads up, only to discover that we were singing the wrong words. I do this so often that I'm not even bothered by it anymore.

Often the changes that have been made communicate more effectively in our modern idiom what the hymn writer intended. But some changes upset me because the elimination of a word, even an old-fashioned word, has weakened the text of the song, robbing it of its power.

One of my favorite hymns is the Lenten hymn written by Johann Heerman and translated by the English poet Robert Bridges: "Ah! Dearest Jesus" (now titled "Ah! Holy Jesus"). The second line of the second stanza used to be "Alas my treason, Jesus, has undone thee." That has been changed to "It is my treason, Lord, that has undone you." To my ear and heart, the difference in the power of those two lines is immense. The word *alas* carries tons of regret and anguish. It has been replaced by the innocuous expletive *it* and the weak little linking verb *is*. I can't understand why. You might say, "Well, obviously *alas* is an obsolete word." Yes. But why then did they not change it in the hymn right across the page, "Alas and Did My Savior Bleed"?

If *alas* is not archaic, was it removed from the song because it expresses too much emotion? Is that also the reason why the second word in the title has been changed from *dearest* to *holy*?

Perhaps a good reason for the change can be given. But my point today about the little word *alas* is that words convey connotative meanings that are powerful, and when they are changed and synonyms are substituted, we don't always end up with the same thing we had before. In fact, I have heard some language experts insist that there is no such thing as an exact synonym in the English language.

If *alas* is archaic, I wonder what we can substitute for it. I can't think of anything at all. "Oh, my?" "Shucks?" "Dear me?" We could speculate as to why we have no modern equivalent for *alas*: perhaps we live in an age where the expression of guilt and anguish over sins or even mistakes is simply not a significant factor in our lives. Perhaps.

In any case, it is surprising to note that the word *alas* did not, in its original usage, convey deep anguish. That seems to have developed over time. *Alas* comes from the Latin *lassus* from which we get our English word *lassitude* and which originally was an exclamation of weariness. *Ah* combined with the *las* of *lassus* meant "how boring" or "how wearisome." But over the years it came to be an expression of grief or anguish—and a very powerful one.

Angle

Sometimes we hear a child misuse a word so creatively that we think perhaps the child's made-up word is more apt than the actual word she intended. A few years ago when one of my nephews was about four years old, he used a word in this way. His father, a fisherman, took his son perch fishing in their boat, and when they came to the right spot, they dropped the anchor. Later, when they were ready to leave, the little boy, realizing that they had not pulled up the anchor, shouted, "Dad, you want me to pull up the yanker?" There you have it: the perfect word. What do you do when you pull up the anchor? You give a yank. If you have fished in one place for a while, the anchor is usually embedded in weeds or mud, and it requires a good firm yank to free it from the lake bottom. So the boy sensibly calls it a yanker.

Of course *yank* has nothing to do with *anchor*. But if we pull the word *anchor* from the murky water of the distant past, we find it makes some remarkable connections to other words in our language, including the name of our language, English.

We borrowed *anchor* from Latin via the Greeks but it goes back, ultimately, to an Indo-European base, *angg*, meaning "bent." Now here's where we get to the name of our language. In the fifth and sixth century a group of people called the Angles lived in an area of the Jutland peninsula (in Northern Europe) that was shaped like a hook. Because the land was shaped like a hook, the Germans called this land *angul*. Eventually these Angles migrated to Britain and the area that they lived in was called Angle-land (England). Thus we see that the very word *English (Anglish)* comes from a word that means bent, angled.

The English abbot and writer Aelfric tells how Pope Gregory decided to send missionaries to convert the Anglo-Saxons to Christianity after seeing Anglo-Saxon slave boys in Rome. Pope Gregory asked the name of the people from whence they came and he was told, "Angles." Then he said, "Rightly are they called angles, for they have the beauty of angels...."

But, to get back to the anchor story, an anchor has an angle to it, a bend, much like a fishhook or a double fishhook, and hence its connection to *angg*, the Indo-European word for bent.

The title of that great classic on the art of fishing, *The Compleat Angler* by Izaak Walton, also derives from this word meaning "bent." Earlier in England an *angle* was a fishhook, and eventually it came to refer to fishing line and rod. In the King James translation of Isaiah 19:8 we read: "The fishers also shall mourn, and all they that cast angle into the brook shall lament."

Ah, Isaiah, how well you knew. Fishers ever since have been lamenting and mourning as they drew their angles in with no fish on them.

Assassin

> Apparently with no surprise
> To any passing Flower
> The Frost beheads it at its play—
> In accidental power—
>
> The blond Assassin passes on—
> The Sun appears unmoved
> To measure off another Day
> For an Approving God.

This seemingly mild little ditty by Emily Dickinson is actually a poem that packs a terrific wallop, raising questions about the nature of a God who allows beautiful flowers to be cut down by a sudden frost while still beautiful. Something in the matter-of-fact nature with which Dickinson narrates this assassination makes me gasp. Especially when I discover that she wrote the poem shortly after the sudden death of a young relative. But I'm not going to explicate the poem today; rather, I will talk about one word she uses in this poem—*assassin*. Dickinson calls the frost that kills the flower at its play an assassin.

Assassin ... assassin. Say it out loud. It makes a satisfying, sinister sound, evil almost. It sounds like the kind of word the pathetic Gollum from

Tolkien's *Lord of the Rings* would use. *Assassin* my press-cious. And it *is* an evil word.

I remember as a boy my fascination with the story in Judges of the God-appointed, left-handed assassin, Ehud, who thrust his dagger so far into the belly of Moabite king Eglon that the fat closed over the blade and he could not get it out. Ehud fits the definition of *assassin* in the *Oxford English Dictionary:* "One who undertakes to put another to death by treacherous violence."

But it was not always that way. *Assassin* comes from the Arabic word *hashshashin,* which means "someone who is addicted hashish" (or marijuana). In Arabic the word *assassin* referred to the Ismaili sectarians who used to intoxicate themselves on hashish or hemp when they were preparing to dispatch some king or public man, or when they were preparing for battle. The Mohammedan Order of Assassins, founded circa 1090, flourished during the Crusades. Its members got drunk on Hashish before they went out to slay Christians. Interestingly, Shakespeare coined the English word *assassinate.*

Through the years *assassin* has lost its drug connotations, but it is still reserved for a select group of people. In English and American speech we use the word to refer to those who murder important people: presidents, rock stars, etc. And Emily Dickinson, when she uses it to describe sudden and unexpected death, not only of flowers by the frost, but also of small children by disease, raises profound theological questions.

Awesome

Recently I heard a speaker suggest that the word *awesome,* a popular exclamation of our day, is not really a very good word to describe our God Jahweh. *Terrible,* he suggested, would much more effectively catch the meaning of the original language and the attribute of God that *awe* or *awesome* try to get at. He is correct, I think, to this extent: In its modern usage *awesome* has been trivialized, voided of its earlier meaning, by its contemporary application to anything from French fries to ball games to a loud sneeze. The terror has departed from the word. It is really just one more in a chain of words that teen culture has appropriated, words such as *keen, nifty, neat, cool, tough, boss, bad,* and so on. Now mind you, I'm not complaining. It is a fact that language constantly changes, and we could no more stop it than we could stop the earth from turning. And the people who change it most often are the ordinary speakers of the language.

But *awe* as the early English folk used it was probably a stronger word than *terrible*—or at least as strong. The first meaning given in the *Oxford English Dictionary* is "immediate and active fear; terror; dread." The second meaning given is "dread mingled with veneration; reverential or respectful fear." Unfortunately I can't read any of the really ancient written usages from Old English (Old English would sound like a completely foreign language to us). But in 1692, John Milton in *Paradise Regained* wrote of Christ: "To His great baptism flocked with awe the regions round."

Interestingly, Milton spells *awe* a-w-e, just the way we spell it. But in a version of Psalm 89:30 from 1300, it is spelled in the Old English way, a-g-h. In that same text, law is spelled l-a-g-h. Now this is an interesting connection, I think. Perhaps you have wondered why some words in English have such odd spellings. Why is there a "g" in *ought*, *caught*, *laugh*, *cough*, etc.? Well, the answer is that the guttural "g" sound of the 1300s gradually changed to a "w" sound during the Middle English Period. This was a change that occurred in many words; some kept the "g" spelling, others, like law and awe, dropped it.

But no matter how you spelled it, *awe* was a fearsome state of mind until quite recently. Today when we sing the chorus "Our God is an Awesome God," I'm not sure what our young people are thinking: A cool God? Nifty? If so, we probably ought to quit singing it. Perhaps only people over forty, who remember what *awe* and *awesome* used to mean, should sing the song. It is possible that a slang usage like "awesome" will diminish in influence and the old meaning will return. More likely though, *awesome* will never again have the power it once had. That's just the way language works. And remember, our God invented language. Awesome.

Bank

I was reading a short piece in *Harpers* magazine the other day in which a father records a number of conversations he has with his son who is in kindergarten. "Dad, can I tell you something? Why do they call a road a road?"

"Son, you know I don't know a whole lot about where words come from. I'm still trying to figure that out for myself."

"Dad, can I tell you something? I know why they call a hotel a hotel. It's because when the whole family gets to the hotel they all start laughing. They laugh *ho*, *ho*, *ho*, and they tell all about. Get it, Dad? Hotel."

7

I enjoyed the piece a good deal because it reminded me of the kind of things my children used to ask or say. It's the kind of question my son was exploring when as a first-grader he wrote this little poem:

> Pop, pop, pop
> Popping popcorn makes me think
> That popping popcorn needs a drink
> Of pop, pop, pop.

He recognized the different meanings of *pop* and explored them in his poem. I think most children are naturally curious about why words mean what they do and why two words that are spelled and pronounced the same can mean different things.

The little boy in the *Harper's* essay also asks his dad why a bank is a place to get money and the edge of a river. Is there a connection between the edge of a river and the place where we get money? Yes, indeed. You can bank on it.

All the *bank* words come from the Germanic *bangk*. The first meaning was "ridge or bordering slope." From that, the riverbank. And from this raised shelf or ridge in nature, it was a small step to the raised bench or shelf of human construction. Eventually from the French or Italian came the idea of a moneylender's bench, called by the French *banque* and the Italians, *banca*. This led to the idea of a place where money is stored. Picture a man sitting behind a board or counter, perhaps in the town square, the place of business from which he lends money. *Bankrupt* literally means "broken bench" since in earlier times a broken bench or counter represented an insolvent moneylender.

Another related word is *banquet*, which literally means "little bench" and used to mean "a small snack eaten while seated on a bench." Today, of course, a banquet is a grand, extravagant feast. Why did the meaning change? I don't know. But I suspect it was used ironically so often that it took on the ironic meaning. By the time of the *King James Bible* translation (seventeenth century) *banquet* had certainly come to mean "a huge feast." In fact, in Song of Solomon we see *banquet* used as an adjective to describe a kind of house where people gathered to feast: "He brought me to the banqueting house, and his banner over me is love."

What a movement *banquet* makes—from a small bench to a huge feasting house where a thousand people could gather to eat and drink. There's just no telling what a word's going to do.

David Schelhaas

Bewildered

What would the world be, once bereft
Of wet and wildness? Let them be left,
O let them be left, wildness and wet;
Long live the weeds and the wilderness yet.

These words by the great Catholic poet Gerard Manley Hopkins should be taken as a creed for our time: "Long live the weeds and wilderness yet." Unfortunately, many people seem to have a creed that is completely opposite, a creed that says "till more fields, build still more roads, pave parking lots, make malls, more malls, more malls."

As my wife and I were driving along the outskirts of a large city recently and I groaned at the ugliness of the developed landscape, I wondered aloud to her whether those people responsible for developing all the malls and strip malls, for laying the asphalt or pouring the cement for all the parking lots, whether, as they drove through it, their chests expanded with a sense of pride, whether they said to their spouses, "Ah, isn't it lovely," or whether they felt gloomy and depressed by the sight. I think I know the answer to my question, but I am bewildered by it.

Bewildered, meaning "hopelessly confused by something complicated, befuddled, puzzled," is a good word to describe how I feel about this issue of wildness, wilderness. Why is it that some people seem obsessed with taming everything except a few designated park areas where the wilderness is preserved—like old houses that are turned into museums? "Isn't this quaint?" we say to each other. "Look at the workmanship in that hand-carved door!" "So that's what an otter looks like." "And the owl in the cage, lovely."

Is it some misunderstanding of the cultural mandate or manifest destiny, this notion that everything that's weedy, wild, or tangled needs to be touched and shaped by man? Or is it simply a desire to use the creation to make money, to extort from earth and sky and water all the wealth we can? I find it bewildering. I am lost in the complicated paths of nature and culture as they wind through each other.

As you have noticed, the word *bewilder* is connected to *wild* and *wilderness;* all these words come from the Indo-European *ghwelt*, meaning "wild." *Wilderness* first meant "the condition of being a wild animal," but the earliest uses in print refer to wild land.

But how did *bewilder* come to mean "puzzled"? In this way: Early on *bewilder* meant to be lost in a pathless place, a wild place, a wilderness. Captain Cook writes in the mid eighteenth century of men being in an unfrequented wood "in which they might probably be bewildered till night." But at the same time it had moved from that specific usage to a more general usage to denote puzzlement or confusion of any kind. Alexander Pope in his *Essay on Criticism* writes that "some are bewildered in the maze of schools."

And I am bewildered in this maze of malls and urban sprawl.

Blame

I suppose people have always been pretty good at blaming. Adam ate of the forbidden fruit and when questioned by God, blamed not only Eve, but also God. "The woman who thou gavest to be with me, she gave me of the tree and I did eat." What stunning audacity Adam displays: "Your fault, God—you gave me the woman." And Eve, in turn, blames the serpent. Ever since then humans have been playing the blame game.

Blame comes from the same source as the word *blaspheme*, a Greek word meaning "to speak evil." *Blas* is related to *blaptikos* meaning "hurtful"; the Greek *phemos* gives us "speak." The meaning of the word *blaspheme* has remained stable since its first usage, but *blame* has come to mean "reproach or censure" and has changed in form over the centuries.

Our present culture is as good at blaming as any in history. How refreshing it would be if a CEO from Enron or WorldCom or any one of a hundred other corporations, caught in situations of destructive lawlessness, would step up and say, "I'm to blame. I'm the one in charge and so the buck stops with me. I take all blame for the evil that was done by my company." How unusual it is for us to hear a leader—a president, a preacher, a professor—say, "My mistake." We not only play the blame game, but we use the word *blame* rather frequently in our day-to-day language.

We also blaspheme as often today as any time in history. But we don't talk about it much. *Blaspheme* rarely pops up in our speech or writing these days because as a culture we have forgotten the very idea of blasphemy. To blaspheme is "to speak irreverently of or utter impiety against God or anything sacred" according to the *Oxford English Dictionary*. And our culture holds very little sacred these days.

When I was growing up as a member of the Christian Reformed Church, a denomination of Dutch ethnicity, we used the Dutch word *spot* or *spotten* to describe irreverent talk about God. And when adults chastised us children for *spotten*, they were serious. God was not to be made light of. *Spotten* is not an exact synonym for *blaspheme*. Broader in meaning, *spotten*

ally accepted authors made up the canon. The canon was created, I suspect, by college professors and the makers of literature textbooks. If an author made it into the college English classroom or the textbook, he—and he usually was a "he"—made it into the canon.

I am, of course, speaking of the canon spelled *canon*. The earliest meaning of the word in our language is "rule" or "ecclesiastical rule." And if we take it back far enough, it comes from a Greek word meaning "reed." Apparently the reed was a kind of measuring stick that was of a standard size. Some have suggested it can also mean "level."

Most of us know of a canon that *is* absolute, that allows for no new admissions, something consciously created to be absolutely exclusive. And this is the canon of Holy Scripture. Over a period of several hundred years after the death and resurrection of Christ, church leaders struggled over the question of which books were the inspired Word of God. As controversies arose, they wrote letters, advised one another, and sought to build consensus. Eventually, councils were held at which the representatives sought to determine which books, letters, and visions were the inspired Word of God and which were merely human constructs. When the councils selected the books, the representatives at these councils used certain rules, certain criteria that a book or letter had to meet before it could be included in the canon of Holy Scripture.

Three criteria especially had to be met for a book to be included in the New Testament:

First, the book had to be written by an eyewitness, that is, someone who had been with Jesus or had seen him. For Paul, this criterion was met by his conversion on the Damascus road. Secondly, the book or letter must have had widespread acceptance in the churches represented at the council. And third, the book had to be compatible with the rest of the scriptures. Thus the letter written by the apostle James occasioned spirited debate because of its unusually strong emphasis on works rather than grace. In the end, of course, it was included.

The word *canon*, let me say again, means "rule, law, criterion." And it is a matter of wonder and mystery to me that the elders and church leaders who devised the rules with which the books of the Bible had to comply and who determined which books did indeed comply were inspired by the Holy Spirit every bit as much as the writers of the books.

The literary canon will never be much of a canon as it changes with the ebb and flow of culture. But the biblical canon is inviolate. We bet our lives on it.

veloped. Most of us know that the prefix *in* can mean "not" (as in *insensitive*), but often it is an intensifier, and it means something like "very," which is the case with the *in* of *incandescent*. It suggests a very white and shining light.

While we're on the subject of candidates, we might as well take a look at the word *senate*. Senate and senator come from the Latin word *senex*, meaning "old." The Roman senate was the council of elders. I suppose that the average age of the senators in the United States Senate is significantly higher than the average age of the members of the House of Representatives, so perhaps it is, to some degree, true to the early meaning of the word.

I'm not sure we can say our use of the word *congress*, however, is true to its Latin meaning. *Congress* comes from the Latin *congressus*, meaning "a walking or coming together." When I have observed the congress, I have seen much more division and partisanship than I have a walking and coming together.

Candidates, senators, congress people–all are frail human beings prone to sin. None can dress in white-robed splendor. For that we will have to wait for the New Heaven and New Earth. In the book of Revelation the Apostle John gives us a vision of the angels and the elders and the throngs of the redeemed all robed in white. What an incandescent sight that will be: "The city will not need the sun or the moon to shine on it, for the glory of God gives it light, and the Lamb is its lamp."

Canon

What do Shakespeare, Milton, Emerson, Hawthorne, and Hemingway have in common? Well, of course, they were authors, writers who wrote poetry and fiction and essays in the English language. Moreover, they are all in the canon. More than that, they are, like most authors in the canon, DWM's. What are DWM's? Dead White Males. Most authors in the literary canon are–or perhaps I should say, were–dead white males. I say *were* because the canon has been changing over the last twenty years. Women writers and non-white writers are increasingly being included in the canon. That's good, but this inclusion has created a problem of sorts. Which women writers, which non-white writers, should be included? And which DWM's should be excluded? If there is no agreement, then there is no longer a canon.

The literary canon, supposedly was created by requiring that any work of literature admitted to the canon meet certain standards, certain laws of literary excellence. Of course, no absolute canon ever existed, but certain gener-

caust. But that use, it seems to me, occurs less and less frequently, and the use of the word with a capital "H" describing Hitler's massacre of the Jews is almost the only usage we see of the word these days. It has become The Holocaust.

In ancient Greek, a holocaust was a sacrifice offered to a pagan god, *holo* meaning "whole" and *kaustos* meaning "burnt." Literally, then, it means "burnt whole." So when Odysseus offered an entire bull in sacrifice to Zeus, that was a holocaust. This idea of a whole burning, an entire burning, is apparent in our use of the word to describe a whole city in flames. And, since large numbers of Jews were burnt in huge ovens, the use of the word to describe that terrible, terrible burning is also apparent. It also suggests Hitler's attempt to eradicate an entire ethnic group.

Both *holocaust* and *bonfire* are words that describe the burning of bones. However, one of them, *bonfire*, has been voided of all terror while the other, *holocaust*, has become a word that brings the most horrid images to our minds.

Candidate

As I look out of my office window, I see sky and the tops of trees. That's because a foot of snow sits on the outside sill of my window, blocking most of my view. The world is blanketed in snow, giving off an incandescent glow; in Latin that would be *candidatus*, white-robed. The world is white-robed this morning.

Roman men who were seeking office had to wear white robes, *candidates*, to indicate to the people who saw them in the street that they were running for office. This was before newspapers and TV, after all, and the people needed some way to identify them. Of course, the symbolism of the white robe might be considered a bit ironic—at least if Roman politicians, like some of ours, were not exactly snow-white in character or behavior.

A related word, *candid*, has an equally ironic connotation when applied to certain political candidates. *Candid* means "white," but also "open and frank." Yet one thing almost all candidates excel at is the art of obfuscation, of muddying an issue, so that their answers are not open and frank, but guarded and ambiguous. How strange that those people we call candidates are often the very least candid of people.

A third word from this same root is one I used a moment ago to describe the glowing snow—*incandescent*, meaning "white and shining"—the word Thomas Edison used to describe the first electric light bulbs he decan mean to joke or tell an off-color story as well as to speak irreverently about sacred things. Still, *spotten* was considered sinful.

But as I said, in our culture, nothing's sacred. Contemporary writer Annie Dillard says in "Teaching a Stone to Talk": "God used to rage at the Israelites for frequenting sacred groves. I wish I could find one.... Now the whole world seems not-holy. We have drained the light from the boughs in the sacred grove."

Bonfire

If you had a large pile of debris—wood and brush especially—and you wanted to dispose of it, you might, if you lived in a rural area, set it on fire. And you would probably call it a bonfire. When Samuel Johnson wrote his famous dictionary in 1755, he assumed that the *bon* of bonfire came from the Latin *bonus* meaning "good," so for him the word meant "good fire." But he was wrong. The origin of the *bon* in *bonfire* is the word *bone*.

When England was still a pagan land, the bones of human corpses were burned at large public fires several times a year. Writing in 1658, the English clergyman Thomas Browne notes that when Christianity was completely established, these sepulchral bone fires were discontinued. But apparently the burning of animal bones in large, festive, public bonfires continued until the late nineteenth century, sometimes to celebrate Midsummer's Eve. And they were sometimes associated with Church holy days. B. Goodge writes in 1570, "Then doth the ioyfull feast of John the Baptist take his turne, when bonfiers great with loftie flame in every town doe burn." So while Johnson was wrong about the origin of the word *bonfire*, he probably came to his conclusion because in his time the fires were probably good and joyous occasions.

Today bonfires—not of bones but of wood and brush—are still occasionally used for celebratory occasions. In the fifties, when I was a boy, the public high school in my hometown had a festive bonfire the night before the big game in which a straw reconstruction of the opposing team's mascot was probably burned and lots of rah-rah speeches were given.

Holocaust is another word that describes a kind of burning. Today when we use the word *holocaust*, we usually use it to refer to the murder of more than six million Jews by Hitler during World War II. It is also used to describe destruction, especially by fire, on a large scale. Thus the firebombing by Allied troops of the German city of Dresden could also be called a holo-

David Schelhaas

Carnation

I was reading the irreverent *Diaries of Adam and Eve* by Mark Twain recently and ran across a passage in which Eve wonders why the saber-toothed tiger has teeth that look like they were made for ripping and eating flesh and yet eats only growing things. Twain is, of course, questioning the idea that prior to the fall there was no death since carnivorous animals must have existed prior to the fall. I will not try to answer his question here, but I do want to explore that word *carnivorous* a bit.

The *carn* of *carnivorous* comes from the Latin word *caro* meaning "flesh." The last part of the word comes from the same root as *devour* so that taken as a whole the word means "flesh devourer."

The *carn* of carnivorous appears in a number of interesting words, for example, the word *carnal*, which means "of the flesh or fleshly" and often is used in combination with the word *knowledge* to indicate sexual knowledge or relations.

The word *carnival* means literally "raising flesh," and referred originally to the practice, during Lent, of eliminating meat, that is, flesh, from one's diet. Few words in our language have traveled further from their original meaning than this word. To many the word suggests wildly decadent celebrations such as Mardi Gras in New Orleans, celebrations which, incidentally, often have their origins in religious festivals. For me, the word *carnival* brings memories of the arrival in my town of a touring group of people who set up Ferris wheels and tilt-a-whirls and octopuses as well as booths in which you could throw rings or knock down bottles to win teddy bears and canes and other cheap and gaudy prizes. The gypsy-like people who traveled with the carnival were called carnies. Few days in my small town childhood were as exciting as the day the carnival came to town. But it had nothing to do with any religious celebration. In fact, the carny folk were thought to be about as far from Christianity as people could be.

Two words associated with death also derive from the Latin *caro*: *Carrion*, meaning decaying flesh, and often more specifically today, road-kill; and *charnel house* which was a place in which dead bodies and bones were deposited. At one time *charnel* meant "cemetery."

Our final *carn* word is *carnation*, which meant in French, "pink or flesh-colored flower." Gjertrud Snackenberg has a splendid poem, "Supernatural Love," in which she tells the story of a small girl who calls carnations "Christ flowers." The girl's father, in an attempt to understand why his daughter calls them Christ flowers, looks the word up in a dictionary where

15

he reads that the carnation is "a pink or flesh-colored variety of Clove." He than looks up *clove* and discovers it derives from *clou*, the French word for "nail." And suddenly for him, "The incarnation blossoms, flesh and nail," and he understands why his daughter calls them Christ-flowers–though he does not understand how she could have known what he discovered–the connection between Christ's flesh and the nails that pin him to the cross. That remains mystery, but then, so much of faith is mystery. And words, especially the One made flesh, but also the many that we employ in our writing and talking, are full of mystery.

Carp

On a recent canoe trip down the Rock River, my partner and I noticed some flopping and splashing in a pool just off the river but connected to the river by a thin channel. We navigated our canoe up the channel and cast our fishing lines into the pool. Nothing happened. No fish rose to our bait. But suddenly we noticed a banging on the bottom of our canoe and then we saw large yellow carp scuttling through the channel where we had "parked" and heading back to the main river. They were huge–eight to ten pounds–and our friend in the canoe behind us stuck out his dip net and netted a couple of them. What to do then? They were too large to lie in the bottom of the canoe, so he finally returned them to the water.

But he did not do it willingly, for he thought they would taste wonderful as smoked carp, and he spent a bit of time carping about our failure to bring an adequate stringer along. Of course, most people today would turn away in disgust from eating carp, but my friend in wanting to save them and eat them was in pretty good company. None other than the writer of the original classic on fishing, Izaak Walton, in his book *The Compleat Angler*, writes, "The Carp is the Queen of Rivers: a stately, a good, and a very subtle fish."

If you have been paying close attention, you may have noticed that I used the word *carp* in two ways–as the fish (a noun) and as a verb meaning "to complain." Is there a connection between the two words? No. The source of the word for the carp fish is unknown though it comes most recently from the Latin *carpa*. The fish must have been available over a wide area, for according to the *Oxford English Dictionary*, "the same name appears in the Romanic, Celtic, Teutonic, and Slavic."

The verb meaning "to complain or to slander" is more interesting to me. It comes from the Latin *carpere*, which means "to pluck." The connection to slander here seems obvious. Figuratively, to pluck at something or pick at it would mean to attack it or slander it. From slander, it is easy to move in meaning to complain.

This Latin verb *carpere* appears in other familiar words. A carpet, for example, was a thick woolen cloth made by plucking or carding wool. The second syllable of the word *excerpt* is also from *carpere*. An excerpt is, of course, a short passage that has been plucked out, something chosen from the whole.

Finally, there is that Latin phrase, *carpe diem*, which has almost become standard English–thanks to the movie *Dead Poets Society*. *Carpe diem* means "seize the day," that is, pluck the day, grasp the moment, live right now. English poets of the seventeenth century often used the *carpe diem* argument to woo young women: "Come, my Celia, let us prove,/While we can, the sports of love." There's something pagan about using the *carpe diem* argument for seduction, but the Bible frequently uses the *carpe diem* idea–from Joshua saying "Choose you this day whom you will serve," to Christ saying, "Today if you would hear my voice, harden not your hearts," to Paul saying, "Now is the day of salvation."

Or even–who was it?–Peter, saying, "I go a-fishing." Of course we're pretty sure it wasn't carp fishing.

Catastrophe

I read the word *catastrophe* the other day and I wondered whether it was in any way connected to *apostrophe*, that little punctuation mark that indicates the absence of a letter. I discovered that, indeed, the two are closely related. *Apostrophe* means literally "turn away," and the punctuation mark indicates that a letter has been omitted, turned away. Similarly, the poetic form called the Apostrophe is a poem written to someone who is absent, usually dead, or to something non-human like the ocean, which cannot comprehend.

Catastrophe literally means "turned over." And that's what a catastrophe is, isn't it? A turning upside down of what is normal: a tornado or a flood or a car accident. Strange that the word for a tiny punctuation mark and the word for huge disasters are almost identical and have nearly identical roots. It reminds one of Mark Twain's remark that the difference between the right word and the almost right word is like the difference between lightning and the lightning bug.

I recently read novelist Don DeLillo's novel *White Noise*, a satire on our modern technological society, and he writes about our need for catastrophe:

> We need an occasional catastrophe to break up the incessant bombardment of information....The flow is constant....Words, pictures, numbers, facts, graphics, statistics, specks, waves, particles, motes. Only catastrophe gets our attention. We want them, we need them, we depend on them. As long as they happen somewhere else. This is where California comes in. Mud slides, brush fires, coastal erosion, earthquakes, mass killings, etcetera. We can relax and enjoy these disasters because in our hearts we feel that California deserves what it gets.

As I said, this novel is a satire, but you can tell it is a perceptive satire, indirectly criticizing our love of catastrophe and our ability to distance ourselves from it via television. The lords of the media, recognizing our need for catastrophe, keep us jumping from catastrophe to catastrophe. Although the media held on to 9/11 longer than usual, they realized that it could only keep our attention for a limited time. But then came anthrax and after that the abduction of a little girl in Salt Lake City and after that forest fires and after that the slaughter of a million people in The Congo and after that the West Nile Virus. For most of us, catastrophe all happens "out there."

St. Luke writes that the gospel of Jesus Christ "turned the world upside down"; in other words, it was catastrophic. But it is a catastrophe not of death and slaughter but of new life and love.

Cell

As I sit here in my office at Dordt College, I can look out of a large window to see a giant maple tree, twenty-three feet around at its base. (I know because I measured its circumference last year.) A bit to the south of the maple is a large elm and then closer to me, a pin oak. It must certainly be as lovely a view as you could find from any window in Sioux Center—though the view from the Sioux Center cemetery, southeast toward Orange City is, perhaps, superior, as splendid a view as any mountain vista—at least to the eye that has learned to see the beauty of a rolling prairie.

But I'm getting sidetracked.

The view from my office is wonderful, and my office itself is a delight, ten feet by twelve feet and opening on to a spacious anteroom that is part of the English Department pod. (I tell you this because it was not always so.) Up until a few years ago, most of the faculty here operated out of wee, windowless offices, spaces we often compared to monks' cells. And that takes us to our word for today, *cell*.

Cell comes from an Indo-European base *kel* and came into the English language via the Latin word *celle* meaning "a small room." Early on *cell* was used to refer to a small monastery next to the main one. Of course, eventually it came to mean "a small chamber in the monastery or a chamber occupied by a hermit."

Other small rooms eventually were also called cells. More than one poet has used *cell* to describe the grave. Thomas Gray writes in his "Elegy in a Country Churchyard": "Each in his narrow cell forever laid."

One of the compartments in the comb of wax made by bees is also called a cell. According to the *Oxford English Dictionary*, some scholars would connect the Latin *celle* with *cera*, wax, regarding the cell of a honeycomb as the original meaning of the word. In a recent *Harpers* article about bees, Susan Brind Morrow connects the cell of the honeybee with the cell of the monk, saying, "The *kellos* of the honeycomb was the cell of the monk."

English poet Louis MacNeice compares books to cells that store the honey of wisdom and knowledge in his poem "The British Museum Reading Room":

> Under the hive-like dome the stooping haunted readers
> Go up and down the alleys, tap the cells of knowledge–
> Honey and wax, the accumulation of years–

In 1672 an English scientist uses the word *cell* as it is used in modern biology, writing of the mass of little cells in an organ.

Many other words derive from that Indo-European root *kel*: *cellar, clandestine, conceal, hall,* and surprisingly, *hell.* Etymologically, both *hell* and *hall* denote "a small hidden place." (Anyone over forty can probably remember that in grade school to be sent out into the hall for misbehavior *was* sort of like being sent to hell.)

But back to the office that I began with. It is a spacious cell, much more a haven than a hell, and I am happy to be here.

Cheer

What town in Iowa has a better name than What Cheer? None. I don't know why its founders called it that, and I don't really care to know because I like to imagine a group of settlers heading for their future home somewhere on this vast sea of grasses called prairie, exhausted by long days of travel, finally reaching this pleasant place, perhaps resting on a meadow or lea from which they can observe a sweetly flowing stream and hear the songs of birds in the evening as they set up camp. "What cheer," someone says to his companions. "What place could be sweeter than this? Let's claim this land and make it our home." And the others quickly agree. "What Cheer," they say to one another, thrilled to have ended their trek and ready to settle the land. What happiness, what joy, what delight and pleasure and good will. What Cheer.

In John Wycliffe's translation of the scripture made in the late 1300s, the word *cheer* is used on several occasions as a synonym for face. Exodus 25:20, for example, describes the cherubim as they turn their faces, that is, their "cheeres," toward the mercy seat. Two hundred years later, Shakespeare wrote in *A Midsummer's Night's Dream*, "All fancy sicke she is and pale of cheere." In other words "pale of face." *Cheer's* first meaning was, indeed, "face," coming, it is surmised, from the Latin *cara*, meaning "face."

But, as early as the sixteenth century the phrase "what cheer" was used to mean "cheer up" or "be of good cheer." It was also used back then to mean something like "What's your mood?" or "What's up?" "What cheer, my love?" says Theseus to Hippolyta in *A Midsummer Night's Dream*.

It is not hard to figure out how the word *cheer* moved from meaning "face" to meaning "happiness." "Be of good cheer" meant quite literally, "Put on a happy face." Eventually this word for face became a metaphor for a particular attitude, one of joy and delight. Then farther down the road it became a verb that meant "to shout out words of encouragement." These days we call the boisterous shouting we do to urge on our teams "cheering." We even have cheerleaders to help us do that.

Sometimes the Spirit of God acts as a cheerleader to the people of God. "Be of good cheer," our Lord said to St. Paul in the King James version of Acts 23:11 as God came to him in a vision by night when Paul was being harassed in Jerusalem. "Thou must bear witness to me in Rome." "Be of good cheer" echoes through the New Testament as St. Paul and other apostles pass on these encouraging words of God.

But it is not a phrase we employ often these days. "Cheer up," we may say to someone who is down in the dumps. But as a general phrase of encouragement, the best we can manage is "Have a good day." I think I prefer "Be of good cheer."

Or better yet, "What Cheer!"

David Schelhaas

Chorus

Most of the time when we use the word *chorus* we use it to refer to a group of people who sing together or to refer to a refrain, a section of a song that is repeated after each verse. If one is into classical theatre, one knows that the Chorus in Greek theatre is a group of actors who move and/or sing together. Sometimes it represented the townspeople, sometimes it took the side of a particular character. The chorus functioned as a character in the play.

Actually Greek theatre started with just the chorus, a group of people—or priests—who sang and danced in praise of their god Dionysius. The Greek word *choros* is usually said to mean "dance." Thus we have the word *choreography*, which means, literally, "the written notation of a dance," the art of representing dancing with signs as we represent singing with notes.

A related Greek word, *chora*, means place. Now *topos* is one Greek word for place—and it is used in a word like *topography*. It's a very literal, scientific kind of word. But, I'm told, Plato actually preferred the word *chora* when he talked about place as a source of energy and power. "Place (*chora*)," said Plato, "is the wet nurse, suckler, and fueler of all things." What Plato meant, according to Dr. Beldon Lane, is that place contains a sort of energy and power for the people within it. According to Dr. Lane, the word *choreography* ultimately comes from this word. And dancing in a place is the deepest way of experiencing the powerful connectedness between people and place.

I think there's something to this notion—that people who live in a place for a long time acquire a relationship with the place, a connection that feeds the spirit. Many people in our current vagabond society are missing out on an essential relationship. They may dance, but they are dancing a disconnected dance.

The captive children of Israel experience that disconnectedness, and they lament, "How shall we sing the songs of the Lord in a strange land?" But when they return to their homeland, their "mouth is filled with laughter, and their tongues with singing."

Cleave

A friend gave me this puzzler the other day: Name two words, spelled the same, pronounced the same, yet defined as almost exact opposites. Well, of course you know; you looked at the title of this piece.

We all know these words though the meaning of one is a bit more archaic than the meaning of the other. We know that a cleaver is a strong sharp instrument used to chop something in two, and the verb *cleave* means "to separate, to cut in two." We see variations of this meaning in words like *cloven*, *cleft*, and *cleavage*. *Cloven* suggests a split, as in the cloven hoof of a goat. *Cleft* suggests an indentation that divides two parts as in a cleft chin or a cleft in a rock. And *cleavage* is a gap or space between two things. This *cleave* comes from the Old English, *cleofan*, which means "to cut or separate."

It is different from the Old English *cleofian*, from which the other *cleave* is taken. It means "to adhere, to be faithful, to stick fast"—not separate or cut, but hold together. The word *clay* comes from the same root. This *cleave* is used less frequently than the other, but those of us who know the *King James Bible* are well aware of this meaning also. Job 29: 10 says, "The voices of the nobles were hushed and their tongues cleaved to the roof of their mouths." And in the Sermon on the Mount, Jesus says, "No man can serve two masters for either he will hate the one and love the other or else cleave to the one and despise the other." An old version of Christian marriage vows describes the newly married couple as cleaving to one another.

As far as the "chopping" *cleave* is concerned, there are also numerous uses of that in older Bible translations such as in Genesis 22:3 of the King James Version: "Abraham clave [past tense of *cleave*] the wood for the burnt offering." In *Paradise Regained* John Milton describes God's action of separating the Red Sea and the Jordan for the children of Israel thus: "As the Red Sea and the Jordan once he cleft."

Of the two meanings, I find the one meaning "to hold on to" less frequently used. That's too bad. We should hang on to it. Cleave to it.

Clerk

My father was a small town merchant, a storekeeper. The people who worked for him were most often called clerks, but also, unfortunately, hired girls. Some of them were middle-aged women, but in the store they were hired girls. Just as an aside, let me note that when people complain about political correctness, they sometimes forget that this movement to use non-offensive language about gender and race has produced many good results. When I think about it now, *hired girl* seems a dreadfully insensitive and inappropriate phrase to describe the women who worked in the store. After all, language has power, and to reduce a mature woman to hired girl is, consciously or unconsciously, a way of keeping her in her place.

Many of us still use the word *clerk* as a designation for those people who work in department stores or grocery stores. We may also have an image in our minds of the clerk as a sort of secretary. Bob Crachit was Scrooge's clerk (or "clark" as they usually pronounce it in the film versions of *The Christmas Carol.*) The secretary of the church council or consistory in many churches is called a clerk. So the word often carries with it the connotation of one who works with pen and paper, a recorder, a note-taker, a writer of information. There's a good reason for this.

The word *clerk* comes from the same source as *cleric* and *clergy*. The OED tells us that "the scholarship of the Middle Ages was practically limited to the clergy, and these performed all the writing, notarial, and secretarial work of the time." Hence the word *clerk* came to be "equivalent to scholar and specially applicable to notary, secretary, recorder, accountant, or penman." Prior to the Reformation, a clerk was a member of any of eight religious orders. After the Reformation its usage broadened to include *any* penman, recorder, or secretary, not necessarily someone in the Church. The original store clerks must certainly have had among their duties the recording of inventories, sales, and so forth.

But where did the word *clerk* or *clergy* originate? That also is an interesting story. In Deuteronomy, we read that the Levites—the churchmen of Israel—are to have "no inheritance among their brethren, for the Lord is their inheritance." The Greek word for *inheritance* is *kleros*. It was used by the early church as a designation for priests and others involved in Christian ministry—*kleros, clericus, clerk, clergy*.

Today, of course, one can be a clerk without being a member of the clergy. But one can hardly be (should not be) a member of the clergy without being a clerk, that is, a writer and scholar. Unfortunately, these days, we do occasionally encounter clergy who are neither scholars nor writers. Often they are preaching on TV.

Common

I was re-reading Peter DeVries's novel *The Blood of the Lamb* recently and came upon this bit of dialogue between the narrator, Don Wanderhope,

23

and his daughter Carol. She says, "Oh, Daddy, you and your beer. It's so common. Nobody drinks beer."

He responds by laughing and then explaining the contradictory nature of her statement. "*Common* means that everybody does something so if nobody does, it's exclusive."

DeVries in this passage is having fun with both of his characters, for he knows that *common* not only means an activity "shared by all," but has taken on as well the connotation of "ordinary, unsophisticated, not quite up to snuff." Something is slightly tainted if it is common.

So both father and daughter are correct in their use of the word, though the daughter's usage does have a context that is humorous.

The word *common* comes from the prefix *com* meaning "together" and the Latin word *munis* meaning "bound." Its most common usage (as I have just shown) is probably as an adjective meaning "ordinary," or "shared by many." But it also has some interesting usages as a noun–though many of them are disappearing from common usage.

Today the noun *common* still functions in our language in places like college campuses where the place that the students come together to eat is called the Commons.

For centuries, peasant farmers in England had fields (called the commons) held in joint occupation, which were not part of the Lord's domain. In early New England, as well, farmers had these commons on which the family cows or sheep might graze. One of the great tragedies of English rural history was enclosure, that is, the fencing in for private use of fields, forests, and meadows owned in common by the inhabitants of a village. Enclosure took these lands away from the peasantry.

This enclosure process brought about the end of the communal existence of the common people. It meant the uprooting of traditional communities. *Common*, remember, comes from two words meaning "bound together," and what better definition is there of *community* than "people who are bound together, held together, by something"?

The first century Jerusalem Christians had all their possessions in common, but it is rare today, outside of the cloister, to find Christians who have all things in common. It is even rare to find people who live in genuine community.

David Schelhaas

Crane

Recently my wife and I journeyed to the Platte River valley around Grand Island and Kearney, Nebraska, to observe the Sand Hill Cranes. It was a marvelous experience. We not only saw lots of cranes, we learned a lot about them. We sat in a blind at dusk on a beautiful spring evening as the sun went down, scattering streaks of pink along the horizon, and watched the cranes settle in on the river by the tens of thousands. Cranes feed in the fields during the day and spend the night standing in the shallow Platte River—safe there from predators. The sounds were as magnificent as the sights. Imagine the sounds of a grade school playground at recess and then imagine what that would sound like if instead of a few hundred children laughing and shouting and playing, you heard thousands. Well, cranes' voices are a bit more raucous than children's, but you get the idea.

We learned that cranes can fly up to five hundred miles a day, that the male and female do beautiful courting dances (we saw these, as well), that they typically have two eggs in their nest, but that one survives and the other dies. We learned that a crane in a zoo in Europe is 93 years old and that at 89 he fathered young. We learned that the shapes of all the letters of the Greek alphabet are patterned after cranes in flight. We also learned about the word *crane*.

Geranos is the Greek word for crane, and our word *geranium* comes from that word because the seedpod of the geranium looks like the head and neck of a crane. It's true. You know how a geranium bloom is made up of a whole bunch of little flowers. Well, before that little flower opens up, it resembles the neck and head of a crane. You can see this resemblance most clearly if you look at a bloom with all but a few of the little flowers already open. Those few at the bottom of the bloom are craning their necks, looking very much like the neck and head of a crane.

I just used *crane* as a verb, and that usage comes from the image of the crane as well. When we crane our necks, we arch them like a crane would. And of course the mechanical crane used in construction also images the bird.

The word *pedigree* also comes from the Greek *geranos* combined with the prefix *pedi* meaning "foot." So, *pedigree* means "foot of a crane" and it describes the shape made by the lines of a genealogical chart.

And finally there is the crane-berry. When the pilgrims in New England saw a berry-bearing plant growing in the bogs that had a stamen resembling the beak of a crane, guess what they called it? Right, cranberry.

25

As I watched the cranes come in at night and take off at 6:50 in the morning, I was struck again by the amazing creative power of our God—and also by the way He has equipped his creatures to care for themselves. The heavens declare the glory of God, not only when we look at the stars but also when we look at the skies filled with birds. The intricacies of creation indicate a creator God. But so do the intricacies of language. How it has unfolded and continues to unfold is a manifestation of God's glory and his involvement in creation.

Crotchety

A friend recently asked me to explain the roots of the word *crotchety*. I am not sure why she wants to know the history of the word. I hope it is not so that she can use it with more vigor as a descriptor of her husband or her boss. Perhaps she, herself, feels crotchety.

The word *crotchet* means "forked or hooked or bent or curved," and it comes from the same root as *crook*, the hooked staff of a shepherd. Those of us who remember grandmothers or aunts who crocheted (pronounced *cro-shayed*) know what the crochet hook (a redundancy) looks like. We can also understand that the robber we call a crook is someone with a bent moral sense. And if we call our husband or wife or boss crotchety, what we are really saying is that he or she has a personality full of little hooks and forks.

I know we usually think of *crotchety* as an adjective with negative connotations. But think for a moment how boring life would be if people were not crotchety, if they were all as smooth and translucent as eggs. So complain, if you like, that your husband demands sweet pickles on his peanut butter sandwich or your wife insists that it is a sin to let a dirty dish sit in the sink overnight, but be just a little thankful for the hooks and curves in our personalities that make us interesting.

Another C word of similar meaning is *curmudgeon*. I have always liked the oxymoron "lovable curmudgeon" but upon closer examination of the word have come to wonder if such a thing as a loveable curmudgeon is possible. The dictionary defines *curmudgeon* as "a surly, ill-mannered, bad-tempered person." In contrast to the crotchety person, nothing is endearing about a curmudgeon.

And little is known about the origin of the word. Dr. Samuel Johnson in his great but idiosyncratic dictionary of the eighteenth century speculated that the word came from the word for heart (*cour*, from which we get *cardiac* and *courage*) and the word *merchent* meaning "evil." But later etymologists, while praising Johnson's inventiveness, disproved his theory.

Another theory is that *curmudgeon* comes from the word *corn* and from a Middle English word, *much-on* or *mich-on* meaning "to pilfer or steal," giving us corn-stealer. But that too has been disproved. The actual origin of the word is unknown.

And now, lest it seem I have been too hard on the crotchety, curmudgeonly older generation, let me conclude with a note on the word *brat*. This word, which originally meant a covering for the body, a cloak or mantle, was later applied in the Old Welsh to the swaddling clothes of infants. Eventually it came to mean "a child."

Today we think of brats as rude, ill-mannered children—young curmudgeons, if you wish. But in the sixteenth and seventeenth centuries, *brat* was a neutral word; it carried no more negative connotation than the word *child* or *youth*. The sixteenth century poet Gascoigne writes, "O Israel, O household of the Lord, O Abraham's brats, O brood of blessed seed."

Bratty kids, crotchety old folks, and curmudgeons, all may be Abraham's brats. There's a comfort.

Daft

The other day, my wife, watching our son-in-law with his large hands gracefully tie the shoelaces of his little daughter's shoes, remarked, "You really are deft." Ever the cynic, I remarked, "He's not only deft, he's daft." I talk that sort of nonsense frequently, but as I said this, I began to wonder. What if *deft* and *daft* come from the same root and once meant the same thing? A quick trip to the dictionary showed that, indeed, they did once mean the same thing. (Though my wife thought me daft when I first suggested it.)

Let me see if I can explain the original meaning and also how *daft* and *deft* came to part company. *Daft* originally meant "mild or gentle." The Middle English *dafte* comes from the Old English *gadaefte* which has as its underlying sense *fit* or *suitable*. Quite likely, mild or gentle people were seen as behaving in a way that was fit and suitable. In the Anglo Saxon translation (c1000) of Matthew 21:5, which we read as "See your King meek, and gentle," the word for gentle is *gadaefte*. In other words, "See your King, meek and daft."

Gradually, however, the mild, gentle meaning descended in connotation to mean "crazy or foolish." First, animals were described as daft, that is, without reason, and eventually people also. The word *silly*, which once meant happy or blessed, slid down the same slope. So that explains where *daft* got its present meaning.

But how does *deft*, meaning "skillful or dexterous," fit into the picture? Again, if we start with the Old English meaning of "fit or suitable," we can see a connection to "skillful." In fact, the root of *gadaefte*, which is *dhabh*, "to fit," carries with it the sense of a joiner or an artisan, someone who skillfully made the ends or corners of a cupboard or piece of furniture fit neatly together. From *fit* to *skillful*, to *dexterous*. Thus we see how one root word meaning "fit" or "suitable" went in two different directions—one meaning "crazy," the other meaning "skillful."

These days it is usually considered much better to be deft than to be daft. But don't be too sure. In the King James translation of the Bible (1611), a translation a bit more modern than the Anglo Saxon version, I Corinthians 3:19 reads as follows: "For the wisdom of this world is foolishness [daftness] with God." It is good to remind ourselves that what the world may call wisdom may seem daft to God.

Diet

In modern Western culture we have almost unlimited access to all kinds and quantities of food, and this easy access has contributed to an epidemic of obesity. But sometimes this abundance of food is countered by another aspect of Western culture, the need to be thin. This emphasis has given rise, as we all know, to medical conditions such as anorexia and bulimia. It has also created heartache in millions of men and women who, because they are not as svelte as movie stars and TV models, are dissatisfied with their bodies. And, it has given rise to hundreds of different diets.

By *diet* I mean, of course, a planned regimen of eating. But that's not the only meaning of *diet*.

One of the great historical stories that I grew up with was that of Martin Luther's heroic defiance of the hierarchy of the Catholic Church. The great climax of that story occurs at the Diet at Worms. As a small child, I had wonderfully horrid visions of a great plate of swirling worms that was placed before Luther like a serving of spaghetti. I knew better, but still how can one not imagine that upon hearing "Diet of Worms." (Later, I heard it pronounced "dee et"; but it seems that both pronunciations are acceptable.)

What was this Diet that Martin Luther attended, and is it connected in any way to this word that now means a "regimen of eating"? Let's go back to the Greek and Latin.

The word *diet* comes from the Greek and then Latin *dieta* meaning "mode of life." Medical writers used the word this way and so it was natural to speak of the "mode of eating" as a *dieta* also.

At some point this usage also became associated with the Latin *dies* meaning "day," and then that meaning was expanded to "a day's work" and a "day's journey," and a "day's food." So that explains our current use of the word: A day's food was a *diet*.

But what about this Diet held in the city of Worms that Martin Luther was forced to attend? I mentioned that the Latin word for *day* influenced the word *diet*. From that we got the meaning of a day fixed for a particular assembly or court to meet. And the word eventually broadened in its meaning to mean a "particular convention or congress." The Diet at Worms was a congress called by the state and which dealt with, among other things, that rebel monk Martin Luther. Here Luther made his famous Roman Catholic-church-defying defense of salvation by grace alone saying, "Hier stehe ich, ich kann nicht anders." ("Here [on this principle of grace] I stand, I can do nothing else.")

Luther is usually pictured as a rather weighty man. We know that he indulged himself in a diet of good German food and beer. But that other Diet, the one at Worms, was in no way self-indulgent, for he put his life on the line in one of the great heroic moments in the history of the Christian church. At least that's my Protestant view on the subject.

Discipline

"The problem with kids today," we hear sometimes, "is that they need more discipline. Parents are too easy on kids–they ought to discipline them more severely. And our schools, what they need to do is employ stricter discipline." As *discipline* is used here it sounds like a pretty nasty thing–almost a synonym for punishment.

"What exactly does *discipline* mean?" someone asked me recently. It comes from the Latin word *discipulus*, "learner," which derives from the verb *discere*, which means "learn." When we think of the word *disciple* we don't usually think of punishment. We think rather of a mentor surrounded by students—Jesus and his closest friends. It is a warm word. Even when we use it as a verb—*to disciple*—it conveys positive action, nurture, and teaching.

But when we move from *disciple* to *discipline* the negative connotations pop up. Not always, of course. If we speak of the academic discipline of English or mathematics, we may think of hard work, but we don't usually think of punishment. Most often, however, when we use the word *discipline*, we think punishment. I had assumed that this was a modern connotation we had given to the word—that it grew with mandatory schooling. But I was wrong.

The use of *discipline* as a synonym for punishment goes way back, probably originating in the church rather than in the school. J. Sergeant in his *History of Monastic Convents*, published in the 1600s, writes, "If any be found unchaste, she receives three disciplines or scourgings." Here *discipline* is a synonym for a whipping. In fact, in the seventeenth century, a whip or scourge used for religious penance was also called a discipline. Sometimes this whip, this discipline, was even studded with nails.

This historical evidence of the word *discipline* used to mean "punish" and even "whip" does not, however, change my intent to use the words *discipline* and *disciple* only with their most positive connotation. Simply to avoid confusion I will call punishment *punishment*, and a whipping a *whipping*. But that loving, shaping, nurturing, teaching, disciplining that parents and teachers do in church, home, and school—that I will call *discipline*.

The word *chaste* has evolved in much the same way as *discipline*. As a noun it means "pure, spotless—and often more particularly—sexually pure." (Interestingly, the word *incest* means literally unchaste, that is, sexually impure.) *Chaste* is a good word. But the verbs *chasten* and *chastise*—now somewhat archaic—meant much the same as discipline: to punish. One of the frequently quoted texts of my childhood, given as an answer to why bad things happen to good people, was Hebrews 12:6, and it was usually quoted from the *King James Bible*: "Whom the Lord loveth he chasteneth, and scourgeth every son whom he receiveth." As a child, I found that text frightening, and even today it brings to my mind an image of God that I don't particularly like. I prefer to think of a God who nurtures, who shapes and purifies his own: Whom the Lord loves, he purifies and disciplines every son (and daughter) whom he receives.

David Schelhaas

Disgruntled

A very popular negative slang word right now is the word *dis*, which is used as a verb and means "to put down, criticize." That makes good sense, for the prefix *dis* has always had a negative meaning. The opposite of *please* is *displease*, and it means literally, "to not please." What interests me today, however, is the large number of *dis* words we have which do not have a positive form; the only word that has survived is the negative *dis* word.

What would you think if, as happened to one of my colleagues a while back, you asked someone how he felt and he said, "Gruntled." Gruntled? Is that good or bad? Let's see, if *disgruntled* means "upset, irritated," then *gruntled* must be good—the opposite of irritated. And it is—however, the word is obsolete. We don't use it any more. But it's a terrific word. It means "content." Can't you just hear someone after a delicious meal, softly grunting in pleasure and satisfaction? Feeling gruntled.

And then there's the word *disgust*. Just this morning one of my colleagues who had been home sick with the flu for two days told me he had been disgusted. Literally. *Goust*, from which *disgust* comes, means "taste." *Disgust* means the opposite, "to sicken, to repel the taste." Again, we don't use the positive form, *gust*, though we do use the word *gusto*, which still means "tasting" or "liking." It has become more generalized in its meaning, however, and is not confined to food but means "zest, enthusiasm, keen liking, excitement." But then, *disgust* has also become more generalized so that today we can be disgusted not just about food but about the weather, our jobs, politics, even our own behavior.

It's curious, isn't it, that we have held on to the negative forms of these words and allowed the positives to become obsolete. Does that say something about our nature, our tendency to focus more on the bad than good? Are we more often disgusted than gusted? More often disgruntled than gruntled? Here's a suggestion: The next time someone asks you how you are feeling, tell her, "Gruntled!"

Dismal

Is any one besides me frequently irritated by TV weather people? One of the things that irks me about them is their tendency to talk and act as if they are in charge of the weather, as if they give us good or bad weather.

31

"What kind of weekend do you have in store for us, Al?" the anchor, playing straight man, will ask.

"Well, I'm going to give you a bit of rain early on Saturday, but then we're going to clear things out on Sunday, and I'm calling for clear skies and moderate temps for most of next week."

Almost as irritating as this pose of being in charge of the weather is the obsequious designation of the weather as "your" weather: "After a short break, Al will be back to tell you about 'your' weather." As if we possess it, like our car or our golf clubs.

E. B. White, in one of his marvelous little pieces from the *New Yorker*, complains about the weather person, whose forecast was "rainy and dismal," because when he used the word *dismal*, he moved from being a reporter and scientific predictor of the weather to a maker of value judgments about the weather by assuming that rain is a bad thing. White says: "The era of pure science was drawing to a close and the day of philosophical science was at hand.... A meteorologist, whose job was simply to examine the instruments in his observatory, had done a quick switch and examined the entrails of birds. In his fumbling way he attempted to predict the impact of the elements on the human spirit."

The word *dismal* is composed of two Latin words, *dies*, meaning "day," and *mali*, meaning "evil," so that literally, it means "bad days." (We see that *mali* root in our words *malefactor*, which means "evil doer," and in *malediction*, which means "evil words or evil speaking.") To speak of dismal days at one time would have been redundant since *dismal* was a noun meaning "evil days." Only later did it become an adjective like *cloudy* or *warm*.

Dismal, at one time, was used to designate the two days of each month that were believed to be unlucky. These days, called Egyptian days because they were believed to have been computed by Egyptian astrologers, were particular, designated days for each month. The evil days for July, according to this system, are July 13 and 22. If you are superstitious, you might want to take note. However, I am happy to say that one of June's supposedly evil days was the sixteenth, a day on which I landed several nice walleye and northern while fishing in Minnesota.

The last chapter of Ecclesiastes begins "Remember now thy Creator in the days of thy youth, while the evil days—*dies mali*—come not, nor the years draw nigh when thou shalt say, I have not pleasure in them." This verse pictures old age as dismal, *dies mali*, evil days. I hope they're not too dreadful since I am rapidly approaching them.

Be that as it may, as I write, the sky is blue, the sun is bright, the neighbor's maple tree fills my entire window with green. It is a good day, *dies boni*.

Easter

I am always surprised at how easily we can use words even when we have no clue about what they mean. For example, last week I went to a Maundy Thursday service. Maundy? What does *Maundy* mean? The question flew around our office, but no one knew. So out came the *Oxford English Dictionary* where we learned that the word comes from the same Latin root as our words *mandate* and *commandment*.

In fact, it is a direct allusion to the Latin translation of John 13:34 in which Christ says, "A new commandment I give to you." In Latin that reads, "*Mandatum novum do vobis.*" This sentence was said at the Last Supper, the occasion at which Christ also washed the feet of his disciples. Many scholars believe that the new commandment—which is "love one another" in John 13:34—really refers to the act of foot washing that Christ performed on this day. Of course, foot washing, as Jesus did it, was a loving act. In any case, Maundy is a shortened form of *mandatum*.

And speaking of unexamined words, what about the word *Easter*? *East* goes back to the Indo-European base *aus*, source of the term meaning both "east" and "dawn." It was also the source of *Austron*, the name of a goddess of the prehistoric Germanic peoples, originally the goddess of dawn. Her English name was Eastre from which our word *Easter* came.

That's somewhat disconcerting, isn't it! The name we Christians give to the day of our most important religious holiday is derived from the name of a Germanic goddess of the dawn. The reason is this: The celebration of Christ's resurrection is celebrated on the first Sunday after the first full moon that occurs after March 21. The key date here is March 21. The feast of the goddess Eastre was celebrated on the vernal equinox, March 21. (I suppose it is also possible that the word *Easter* was carried over to Christianity as part of the Christian missionaries' effort to connect new converts to the familiar.)

Because of this tenuous connection, some Christian leaders do not use the word Easter, but instead speak of Resurrection Sunday. I like that idea but doubt it will take root in our culture.

However we designate the day, the good news is that the Lord is risen. He is risen and has given us a maundy, a mandate, to love one another.

Ecstasy

I teach literature, and sometimes in my literature classes we talk about characters as being either static or dynamic. A dynamic character is one who changes significantly from the beginning of the novel to the end. Pip in Dickens' *Great Expectations* and Scout in Harper Lee's *To Kill A Mockingbird* are examples of characters who move from innocence to experience and emerge at the end of the novel far different from who they were at the beginning. A static character is one who is pretty much the same at the end of the story as he was at the beginning. Characters like Joe Gargary in *Great Expectations* or Atticus Finch in *To Kill a Mockingbird* can be called static because they are not much changed at the end of the novel. The word *static* comes from the Greek *statikos*, meaning "causing to stand."

The word that I'm interested in today is not a related word, *ecstasy*. If I asked what *ecstasy* meant, you would probably answer, "Really, really happy or excited." We might use *ecstasy* to describe the reactions of the winning side at a ball game. We would describe as *ecstatic* the reactions of parents whose lost child is returned to them.

But we sometimes use *ecstasy* in quite different ways. We speak of sexual ecstasy and religious ecstasy. We speak of being in an ecstasy of rage or grief. None of these are really about happiness. This usage leads us to the most basic meaning of *ecstasy*, which has to do with being put out of one's mind. In John Wycliffe's translation of the New Testament, he says of the people who had seen Peter and John heal the lame man (Acts 3:10): "They were filled with wonder and ecstasy."

When your rational self has been displaced by joy or grief or rage or passion, you are experiencing ecstasy. Sometimes we have seen this mindlessness as a loss of contact with reality; at other times it is perceived as a heightened reality. Sometimes it may seem as if we are standing outside of ourselves, looking at ourselves.

How does this meaning fit with the word *static? Static*, remember, comes from a word meaning "causing to stand" or "a place to stand." If we add the *ek* prefix, meaning "out," we have the idea of being put out of a place to stand, being taken out of our mind.

The late Catholic theologian and psychologist Henri Nouwen gives the word a different twist in his book *Lifesigns:* "I consider it very important to reclaim the word *ecstasy* for all Christian people who strive to move from the house of fear to the house of love." Nouwen takes the original etymology of *ecstasy* quite literally and says that it means to move out or away from a static position, away from standing still. People who live ecstatic lives, says Nouwen, "are always moving away from rigidly fixed situations and exploring new, unmapped dimensions of reality." He goes on to suggest that ecstasy is shared life, life in community; static living, by contrast, is individualistic.

I like what Nouwen does with the word *ecstasy;* unfortunately one cannot "reclaim" a word just because it makes sense and fits with his ideas. As far as I know, *ecstasy* never meant in everyday usage what Nouwen wants it to mean, even if it fits with the etymology. I doubt that his meaning of the word will never become a generally accepted meaning.

Eucharist

Eucharist is a word for Holy Communion and also for the consecrated bread and wine of Communion. It is not used much by certain Protestant denominations, but for others, like Lutherans and Episcopalians, it is a common word, especially during Lent. The word comes from a Greek word meaning "to show favor, gratitude, thanksgiving." It refers not only to the fact that during the Last Supper Christ gave thanks, but also to the fact that because of Christ's sacrifice Christians should give thanks, should be most thankful, be more thankful for this than for anything else on earth.

Another word that comes from the same root as *Eucharist* is the word *charisma*. When we use *charisma* today, we usually think of somebody with a wonderfully engaging personality that draws people close, someone with charm and allure. Or we associate the word with pentecostalism, that is, with speaking in tongues or faith-healing. However, in historical Christian theology, *charisma* has been thought of as a divinely inspired gift that might include healing but also such gifts as prophesying or teaching.

It seems obvious that Christ had charisma. After all, as a God-man, he had the spiritual gifts of healing and prophesying. And at the height of his ministry Jesus had immense popularity. People flocked to hear him. They were amazed at his wisdom and the wondrous works he did. They were drawn by his charisma. But the prophet Isaiah tells us he was despised, a person from whom people hid their faces. Do we see this un-charismatic Christ in the New Testament? Yes, for it is Christ in his suffering and dying that Isaiah describes as despised and one from whom people hid their faces. At that time, even Peter hid his face from his Master. Ironically, as Christ was giving us the greatest gift, he was least charismatic in the popular sense of the word.

In celebrating the Last Supper, Christ gave thanks and showed favor. Christians today, as they respond to his gift of life, are still shown favor and given gifts of grace, charisma.

Fete

I play on a hapless, winless faculty basketball team that is part of an intramural program, and today I received an e-mail from our coach which began "Dear unfeated players." I immediately thought I saw a connection between his use of that word and the word *fete*, which means "to praise or honor." We certainly are unfeted, that is, we have not garnered any praise or honor. No celebration has surrounded our play.

So did I make a valid connection? Do *defeated* and *feted* have a root in common? No, they do not. They come from two different roots. But both are interesting.

Defeat means literally "to undo." The *feat* part of the word comes from the Latin *facio*, meaning "to make or do." The primary meaning of *defeat* today, "to conquer," was first used in the sixteenth century, but before that the word meant "ruination or destruction." *Deficit*, *deficient*, and *defect* are also words from this same root, *facio*, with different but related meanings.

That other word I mentioned, *feted*, comes from the same word that *feast* comes from. Most of us probably think of food the minute we see the word *feast*, but the earliest meaning is broader. *Feast* first of all suggests celebration, joyful merriment, and it comes from the Latin *festus*, meaning "joyful." In English it referred to religious celebrations like Easter. *Fete* is the modern French descendent of the Latin word for *feast*, but it still does not carry any suggestion of food with it. When we fete someone, we honor her. The ceremony at which we give honor is also called a *fete*. So the word is both verb and noun.

Of course it was natural for the word to take on the suggestion of food and extravagant eating. What better way to celebrate than with food? *Feast* with its connotation of food occurs already in the 1200s. Chaucer writes in one of his tales: "Full busy was Griselda in everything that to the feast was pertinent," and the clear connotation is that Griselda is preparing food.

Still, I am left in the dark as to what my e-mail meant with the word *un-feated*; I am defeated in my quest to connect it to *fete*. But this I know, our lives consist of both defeats and feasts. If you can manage it, I suggest that you try to have more feasts than defeats as you go through life. As the Preacher says in Ecclesiastes 9: "So I commend the enjoyment of life because nothing is better for a man under the sun than to eat and drink and be glad. Then joy will accompany him in his work all the days of the life God has given him under the sun." What brave and festive words from a dark and gloomy book.

Fret

The majority of the words in the English language are not English, that is, they did not come from the Anglo-Saxons whose language forms the foundation of English. The majority of the words in our language are imports from Latin, words that are usually of several syllables and have prefixes and suffixes. In my last two sentences the words *majority, language, imports, syllable, prefix,* and *suffix* are all from the Latin. (I must note that in frequency of use Ango-Saxon rules: According to Joseph Williams, 83 percent of the 1000 most frequently used words are from Anglo-Saxon roots.)

The Latin words are essential to our language, but I prefer Anglo-Saxon words. They are usually short, often four-letter words. They have more punch, more color. Sometimes, however, I fear that too many are disappearing from our usage. Perhaps this is because we live in a time of linguistic pretension, that is, we use words to show off. The more long words we use, the smarter we think other people think we are. But of course our really fine writers knew better. Ernest Hemingway worked diligently to use the direct Anglo-Saxon words of the language. Robert Frost also. In his great poem "Stopping by Woods on a Snowy Evening," all the words are single syllable words except for fourteen two-syllable words and one three syllable word.

One of those four-letter Anglo-Saxon words that seems to be disappearing from common usage is *fret*. I fret about little things like this; *fret* is such a useful little word. "Fret not thyself because of evil doers," the psalmist writes in Psalm 37. Those words are beautifully set to music in the great alto solo from Mendelssohn's *Elijah* titled "O Rest in the Lord." So I will try not to fret about *fret*. It is noteworthy, though, that *fret* appears at least eight times in the *King James Bible* and only four times in the New International Version.

In the first chapter of I Samuel, we read of Hannah fretting because she does not have any children. God is fretted by those who have known him in their youth and then forgotten him, we are told in Ezekiel 16:43.

The Anglo-Saxon word *fret* meant "to eat up or devour." By the fifteenth century, however, *fret* had evolved to mean "gnaw at (metaphorically), or worry." Actually the older meaning is suggested in Isaiah 8:21. There we read, "and it shall come to pass that when they shall be hungry, they shall fret themselves," that is, devour themselves, feed on themselves.

But, of course, the primary meaning is "to worry." Two other meanings of the word *fret* come from other sources: the fret that is the ridge on the fingerboard of a guitar, and the fret that means an ornamental pattern of straight bars intersecting others at right angles, as in a trellis.

In Shakespeare's play *Hamlet,* Guildenstern has been engaged by the King to use his former friendship with Hamlet to find out what Hamlet is up to. Hamlet realizes that Guildenstern is trying to draw information from him for the sake of the King, and at one point he says to Guildenstern, "Call me what instrument you will, though you can fret me, you cannot play upon me." Shakespeare has made a pun on *fret* using both its musical meaning and the more conventional meaning of irritate or worry.

Here's a parting suggestion. Use the word *fret* in your speech today. Tell your kids not to fret about that math exam. Tell your boss not to fret–that you will get the work done. Let's none of us fret but rest, instead, in the Lord.

Frolic

Before we explore the word *frolic,* I want you to take a brief trip with me to Harmony, Minnesota. In the 1970s seven Amish families bought small farms and settled there, and today over a thousand Amish live in the area. I recently had the opportunity to visit with some of them and tour a number of their farm places.

My visit was most interesting. I found myself at the same time attracted to and repelled by the Amish lifestyle. On the one hand, I saw freedom from television and much of the trashy pop culture of our day. I saw families working together, living in community. I saw polite, smiling children.

But I didn't see anything that looked like a toy. No ball field or backboard anywhere, even by the school. I didn't see much beauty, either. Few flowers (not practical, I guess), no pictures. The schools were bleak, cramped places and the farmyards were a mess. Where does a really curious child go to satisfy her thirst for knowledge, I wondered. Do the children play games? Do the adults have fun, or does life consist entirely of work and worship–*ora et labora*? And then our guide mentioned the barn building fests they have, and he called them *frolics.* How typical, I thought, for these serious people to call a major work bee a party. For that's what a frolic is. A party. A merry making.

The word comes from the German *frölich,* which literally means "gladly." Many of us know the old German Christmas carol "*O du Fröhliche, O du Helige.*"

Actually the first image that comes to my mind when I hear the word *frolic* is children cavorting on the playground. That image derives directly from the earliest meaning that probably goes back to the pre-historic Indo-

European source that meant "spring upward" or "move swiftly." And I suppose that joyful kind of movement might be seen at an Amish barn building. Certainly the barns spring upward quickly.

I'm glad the Amish have frolics. I hope they are joyful occasions. We would all be blessed, I think, if our work was more frolicsome. Walt Whitman has a poem about the joy of physical labor called "I Hear America Singing":

> I hear America singing, the varied carols I hear,
> Those of mechanics, each one singing his as it should be blithe and strong,
> The carpenter singing his as he measures his plank or beam,
> The mason singing his as he makes ready for work or leaves off work,
> The boatman singing what belongs to him in his boat, the deckhand singing on the steamboat deck,
> The shoemaker singing as he sits on his bench, the hatter singing as he stands,
> The wood-cutter's song, the ploughboy's on his way in the morning, or at noon intermission or at sundown,
> The delicious singing of the mother, or of the young wife at work, or of the girl sewing or washing ...
> Singing with open mouths their strong melodious songs.

Sadly, Whitman's picture is obsolete. Fifty years ago in my hometown, Rolly, the Chevy Garage mechanic of my childhood, whistled constantly as he worked. And my father sang frequently as he labored in his small-town grocery store. My grandfather, I'm told, sang Dutch psalms as he took his team and wagon out to deliver milk at 6 A.M. Our culture lost something inestimably profound when it lost, often in the name of efficiency, the concept of joyful work. The Amish, with their barn-raising frolics, have retained it. On the other hand, I think that frolicsome play is equally desirable, and I wish for the children's sake, that the Amish allowed a bit more opportunity for that kind of frolic.

Frugal

In a story by Wendell Berry that I was teaching the other day, I ran across this sentence: "He loved the frugal, ample household run by his mother and his grandmother." "That seems strange," I thought. "How can something be both frugal and ample?" *Ample* means spacious, wide, plentiful; and *frugal* means tight, stingy, limited. Right?

Wrong.

Wrong, as far as *frugal* is concerned. Frugal is a word that has undeservedly come to have a rather negative connotation, as it is often associated with words like *stingy, parsimonious, tight*.

But Webster defines *frugal* as "not wasteful, economical, thrifty, not luxurious." Those are not bad words. The etymology of *frugal* also has a positive emphasis.

The word *frugal* comes from the dative case of the Latin noun *frux* meaning "fruit." To be frugal is to enjoy the fruit of one's labor, the fruit of God's providing, his providence. Now it may almost sound paradoxical to our ears, this linking of *fruit* to *frugal* with its connotations of being economical. John Ayto suggests it probably happened this way: Something that is fruitful or productive is profitable, and to be profitable it must be economical—hence *frugal's* connotation of careful expenditure.

Dr. Stephen Bouma-Prediger gives this definition of *frugality*, which he categorizes as a virtue: It is "the economy of use or efficient use given the limits of the goods available. It is characterized not by the parsimonious wish to hold in or keep back, but rather by a desire to use sparingly that which God has provided in order to allow others to live and flourish. Thus ... frugality represents a form of hospitality."

In a 1965 translation of John Calvin's commentary on Genesis we read, "The custody of the garden was given in charge to Adam to show that we possess the things which God has committed to our hands, on the condition that, being content with the frugal and moderate use of them, we should take care of what shall remain.... Let [man] so feed on its fruits that he neither dissipates it by luxury, nor permits it to be marred or ruined by neglect."

A related word from the same root as *frugal* is the little used word *usufruct*. It is defined in the *Oxford English Dictionary* as "the right of temporary possession, use, or enjoyment of the advantages of property belonging to another, so far as may be had without causing damage or prejudice to this." The word combines two roots, one meaning "to use" and the other from the Latin *fructose* meaning "to enjoy." It describes exactly our relationship to the possessions we have on this earth. Too bad *usufruct* has nearly disappeared from common usage.

And a final word from Proverbs 23:4: "Do not wear yourself out to get rich; have the wisdom to show restraint." Frugality is restraint, not only in the use of the resources God has given us but even in the use of our bodies and minds. We may not dissipate the earth and its resources with luxury. But we may and must use them with joy and gladness in the service of our neighbor and our Maker so that, as Calvin says, "We may hand them down to posterity as we have received them or even better."

David Schelhaas

Furrow

The other day as I was teaching a poem that had the word *furrow* in it, a student raised his hand and asked, "What's a furrow?" I was shocked. The young man was from a small rural community, and I simply couldn't believe that he had never heard of a furrow, seen one, or even, perhaps, plowed one. It turned out that many of the students in the class had not heard of the word *furrow*.

I wondered how this could be since many of these students were from farm communities, so I called one of our agriculture profs, and he explained that to plow a furrow one needs to use a moldboard plow. At one time, he said, up to 80 percent of the plowing done in northwest Iowa was done with moldboard plows. But more recently, most plowing is done with chisel plows. In addition, we have ridge-till and no-till planting. So, he said, it is quite possible to grow up on a farm these days and never see a furrow plowed.

Still, my students, even if they no longer plow furrows, ought to have read about them and gone to the dictionary (with furrowed brow) if they did not understand what they read. The word occurs a number of times in the Bible, sometimes as a metaphor. Thus in the King James version of Psalm 129:3 we read, "The plowers plowed upon my back; they made long their furrows." I would imagine the Psalmist is talking about a whipping, but he calls the lash marks "furrows" and the one who wields the whip a "plower."

Some scholars say that the first syllable of *furrow* derives from the Latin, *versus* which means "to turn." Thus to plough, to turn the soil, is to furrow. Interestingly the word *verse* used to describe poetry comes from the same source, for poetry is a deliberate turning from line to line in a way that prose is not. In fact, the comparison can be made between plowing a furrow and writing a line of poetry, for both require that the plower/poet make a turn and begin another line/furrow. And then another. (I do not find these words linked in the etymology given in the *Oxford English Dictionary*, but I like the connection too much not to mention it.)

I am afraid, however, that this old, old word, *furrow*, may soon be used about as infrequently as the word *furlong*. The *furlong* is an almost archaic measuring term. Today, we only hear the word *furlong* in the context of horse racing where it means an eighth of a mile. The word comes from two words, furrow and long. It stood for "a furrow ploughed across ten acres"– which in England was the length of a standard-sized square field. And it measured about an eighth of a mile, though it was not an exact distance since the acre itself was not consistently of one size.

41

A moment ago I used the words *no-till* and *ridge-till*. That word *till* is also a very old word, but it seems destined to remain an active part of the farmer's vocabulary. The word *till* meant, originally, "striving to obtain a goal." It comes from a prehistoric Germanic word *tilojan*, a derivative of the noun *tilam*, which meant "aim or purpose." After this it came to mean "labor" and from labor came the idea of "cultivating the soil." We might think of it this way: In earlier days, a person's aim was usually labor, and that labor usually involved working with the soil, tilling it. And so the meaning of the word gradually narrowed, moving from a general to a more specific meaning.

The preposition *till* or *until* which means "up to a certain point" seems also to have come from the root that means aim or goal. The fixed point is the goal—whether it be in space or time.

One last meaning of the word *till* is "the drawer or tray for keeping money." One of the enduring pictures in my mind from my childhood is of my father standing over the cash register in his store, cigarette hanging in the corner of his mouth, furrowed brow, counting money at the end of the day. He was, as he said, "checking the till." It would be nice to make an etymological connection between his kind of striving to make a living and the kind that the farmer did as he tilled the field, but no such connection exists. This *till* has origins that, as the *Oxford English Dictionary* says, are "obscure." And that's all it says about its origins.

Gallery

I recently taught Ernest Gaines' fine novel, *A Gathering of Old Men*, and repeatedly the various characters use the word *garry*. Set in Louisiana, the novel has three different groups of characters: Blacks, Cajuns, and Whites of the old southern aristocracy. The Blacks and Cajuns use the word *garry*, and it is clear from the context that a *garry*, whether it is on the plantation owner's mansion or the poorest sharecropper's cabin, is an open porch.

I asked my students what word they thought the word *garry* came from, but none could say. So I told them I thought it was a contraction of *gallery*, but I could not tell them why. When I got out of class, I checked my dictionary of word origins and found that my instincts were correct. The original meaning of gallery in English is "a long roofed walkway or porch along the wall of a building." A present definition of gallery—a place where paintings or sculptures are exhibited—did not develop until the end of the sixteenth century. And I suppose it came because pictures were often exhibited in long, narrow, porch-like rooms. Another current meaning, "a group of people at a sporting event or some other performance," probably derives from the place—a kind of gallery—in which they sit.

But the story of *gallery* meaning "a porch" gets more interesting. The English took the word from the Old French, *galleria*, which came from the Latin *galeria*. I suspect that the word is used in the French Cajun country of Louisiana more because of the French influence than the English.

But here's the amazing part—amazing, at least, if you are surprised at how word meanings change over history. The Latin *galeria* was probably an alteration of the word Galilee. Now how in the world did we get from a province in Palestine to a porch or an art museum?

Well, some old churches had a porch or chapel at the far end of the church building, and apparently this porch was sometimes called Galilee, since it was far away from the main section of the church—just as Galilee was far from Jerusalem. One can imagine some priest, centuries back, saying something like, "Yeah, I hung my coat way over in Galilee."

However it happened, today in Louisiana, open porches with roofs are called *garries*, from the word *gallery*, from the word *galeria* from the word *Galilee*. And it all makes perfectly good sense in a strange, meandering, illogical way.

Gargoyle

Onomatopoeia is one of those words most English teachers love and therefore one that most English students have had to learn to spell and define. It is a word we associate with poetry; it is used to describe a word that imitates the sound of the thing or action that it signifies. Words such as *hush*, *shriek*, *slap*, *boom*, *buzz*, *sizzle*, and a host of others are onomatopoetic. They sound like their meaning.

Gargle is an onomatopoetic word. When we gargle, we hold a liquid suspended and rattling in our throats. The noise that we make in our throats, not really a rattle at all, is best described as a *gargle*. Gargle, gargle, gargle.

Gargle has spawned several other words, one of which is *gargoyle*. We know gargoyles are those "so ugly that they're cute" stone-carved creatures often seen on old buildings, especially cathedrals. I suppose most of us would think that the key fact about gargoyles is that they are these ugly little creatures. In fact, that's the primary meaning of the word today. Novelist

43

Hall Caine talks about gruesome gargoyles carved on a candlestick, and the poet Robert Browning is said to have carved "verbal gargoyles," that is, grotesque descriptive similes and metaphors.

But the primary function of a gargoyle was as a spout at the base of the roof of a building to carry rainwater clear of the walls. And now, you see the real reason they are called gargoyles. It has nothing to do with their ugliness and everything to do with the sound of the water going through the stone gargoyle spout and gushing out of its mouth–the sound of a gurgle or gargle.

A very unpleasant word from our language, *regurgitate*, comes from the same onomatopoetic root. When we think of the sound that usually accompanies regurgitation, we know immediately where the word came from.

But these gargoyles, these ugly little creatures, have a long association with bad and evil things–probably because of their ugliness. The poet Henry Wadsworth Longfellow writes in his sonnet "Divine Commedia ii": "Fiends and dragons on the gargoyled eaves/Watch the dead Christ between the living thieves." Longfellow uses this sonnet to set the tone for his translation of Dante's "Inferno." In other words, hell and gargoyles go together.

Think of that when you take a swig of Listerine tomorrow morning and begin to gargle.

Grass

The early rains and thunderstorms have turned my thoughts and eyes to the ground which was so recently snow-covered and now is beginning to take on a shade of green it did not have a couple of days ago. What is it about grass in the spring that is so cheering? Well, the sign of new life, I suppose, and the beginning of the warm seasons.

The word *grass* means simply "that which grows" and comes from the same root as the word *grow*. That makes sense, for grass constitutes one-quarter of the world's vegetation and is probably our most important plant. More than seven thousand species of grass exist, including bamboo, sugarcane, rice, millet, sorghum, corn, wheat, barley, oats, and rye. But of course when we say *grass* today, we mean the stuff that we grow as our lawns, the plant on which Americans lavish over a million tons of chemical fertilizer a year.

It was not always so. The lush green monoculture lawn, weed-free and uniform as a parking lot, is a rather recent phenomenon that apparently began in England. In the mid-1800s, when the American novelist Nathaniel Hawthorne visited England, the lush green lawn with one species of grass was all the rage. He wrote home that he much preferred the more natural American lawn with its varieties of weeds, nettles, clovers, and dandelions. I have always thought Hawthorne a wise man.

Words, like grasses, as I have noted, have roots, and the words *green* and *graze* come from the same root as the words *grow* and *grass*. *Lawn*, however, is another story. It comes from the Old French *launde*, which is borrowed from the same prehistoric German source as the word *land*. So, like *grass* and *ground*, *lawn* and *land* have the same root.

Carl Sandburg has a fine little poem about the power grass has to cover up and make us forget, how grass, in a sense, destroys historical evidence.

Grass

Pile the bodies high at Austerlitz and Waterloo.
Shovel them under and let me work—
I am the grass; I cover all.

And pile them high at Gettysburg
And pile them high at Ypres and Verdun.
Shovel them under and let me work.
Two years, ten years, and passengers ask the conductor:
What place is this?
Where are we now?

I am the grass.
Let me work.

Another, older poet also wrote a poem about grass. It's recorded in Isaiah 40: 6-8:

The voice said, "Cry."
And he said, "What shall I cry?"

"All flesh is grass
And the goodliness thereof
Is as the flower of the field.

The grass withereth,
The flower fadeth:
Because the spirit of the Lord
Bloweth upon it: Surely,
The people is grass.

> The grass withereth,
> The flower fadeth: But
> The word of our God
> Shall stand forever."

Both poets write in a similar melancholy vein, and both speak prophetically, but Isaiah gives us hope. His withered grass is not the final word: there is still the word of God, and it shall stand forever.

Green

We know that green is the preeminent color of growing things and was formed from the same Germanic base as the word *gro*, which produced the word *grow*. Although green is usually a positive color, it can be used to denote jealousy as Shakespeare uses it in *Othello*: "Beware the green-eyed monster which doth mock the meat it feeds on." Green also indicates immaturity, not only in fruit but also in people.

For most of us most of the time, however, *green* is laden with positive connotations. Because of that and because J. R. R. Tolkien uses the color green to talk about adjectives, I'm going to depart from my usual format today and say a few words about the nature of language. Tolkien writes in his well-known essay "On Fairy Stories":

> The human mind, endowed with the powers of generalization and abstraction, sees not only *green-grass*, discriminating it from other things (and finding it fair to look upon), but sees that it is *green* as well as being *grass*. But how powerful, how stimulating to the very faculty that produced it, was the invention of the adjective: no spell or incantation in Faerie is more potent.

From here, Tolkien goes on to suggest that incantations in faerie land are not that much different from adjectives in the real world: "The mind that thought of *light, heavy, gray, yellow, still, swift*, also conceived of magic that would make heavy things light," that could take the green from the grass and make it a deadly green upon a man's face. Tolkien then goes on to talk of man the myth maker, the writer of fantasies, as a sub-creator. And it is quite possible that he is drawing on Andrew Marvell who, in his poem "The Garden," writes,

> The mind, that ocean where each kind
> Does straight its own resemblance find;
> Yet it creates, transcending these,
> Far other worlds and other seas,
> Annihilating all that's made
> To a green thought in a green shade.

Rather than moving into the green world of the imagination, I want to stay a little longer with the lowly, or perhaps the holy, adjective. How barren would be our language and our lives without adjectives. What a gift it is that we may not only lie down in pastures but that they may be *green* pastures. How trivial and limiting to say that an adjective is merely a modifier, something that changes a noun slightly. Call it rather a transformer. That pasture is not merely pasture; it is fresh, lively, lovely, luxuriant, verdant, rich, nourishing, fruitful, fragrant, pleasant, wholesome—in short, green.

Does a sheep see a "green" pasture? I doubt it. I don't mean that he is color blind, though he may be. What I mean is that I do not think he is able to separate green from pasture. For, as far as we know, a sheep does not have the human capacity for generalization and abstraction and, consequently, does not have a language that is at all like human language.

We don't know how the human mind comes to have innate properties for the acquisition and use of language. Noam Chomsky says we may attribute our ability to use language to evolution so long as we realize that there is no substance for this assertion—it is simply a belief. "When we study human language," says Chomsky, "we are approaching what some might call the 'human essence,' the distinguishing qualities of mind that are, so far as we know, unique to man." Now Chomsky is a rationalist who wants to hold up the autonomous dignity of man against the behaviorists. But what he says suggests to me that the human ability to acquire and use language, including adjectives, to separate green from grass, blue from sky, red from blood, is a deeply embedded creational structure, God-ordained. Seen in that light, the adjective and our ability to use it is something that is set apart for humans, something sanctified.

Take off your shoes; the *green* pasture in which you stand is holy ground.

Hand

There's an old joke in which a person falls into the street and can't get up, so he calls out to a passerby, "Give me a hand, give me a hand." The passerby stares at him for a moment and then begins to applaud.

I know, it's cruel and dumb, but it illustrates something about people and language. We are constantly and almost unconsciously inventing new and creative ways of saying things. To "give a hand" is a creative way of saying "clap for, applaud." It is probably an example of what Aristotle in his *Rhetoric* called metonymy—the substitution of some attributive word or suggestive word for what is actually meant. "Hand" is substituted for what is actually meant, the clapping of hands together to indicate approval.

The word *hand* probably comes from a root meaning "to seize or pursue." The Swedish *hinna* meaning "reach" comes from the same source as does our word *hunt*. The hand, then, was a body part used for pursuing or grasping.

Handsome, which today means good-looking or attractive, at one time meant "easy to handle." A writer in 1598 writes, "Neither were the barbarous huge targets and long pikes so handsome among trees and low shrubs as darts and swords." Later the word came to mean "handy and convenient" and later still "clever and appropriate" as in, "He made a handsome speech in the senate." Then came the meaning applied to a fortune or gift as in, "He made a handsome contribution to the building fund." That meaning is still with us.

But most prevalent today is the meaning of "good-looking." In 1622, Wither writes, "Who could dote on thing so common as meer outward handsome woman?" So it is clear that from early on this meaning existed with the others. What we have had, then, with *handsome*, is a variety of meanings used in the sixteenth and seventeenth centuries gradually narrowing to apply primarily to physical appearance, and that usually of males.

Other *hand* words in the English language have come to us via the Latin. *Manus*, meaning "hand," has given us *manual, manufacture, maneuver, mandate, manipulate, emancipate*, and, I am sure, many others. In *emancipate*, the *e* means "away," the *man* from *manus* means "hand," and the *cipate*, from *capere* means "take." Literally, then, *emancipate* means "take away hand." When Lincoln issued the Emancipation Proclamation he, in effect, said to the slave owner, "Take away your hand." In other words, "free the slaves."

Well, I began with an example of metonymy and I'll end with an example of a similar figure of speech, synecdoche, where a part stands for the whole. Those slaves that were finally emancipated were often called hands, for *hand* suggested their most valuable quality to the slave-owner, the ability to do manual labor. What a tragedy when any human being is reduced to one small part of the total human potential suggested by the phrase "created in the image of God."

David Schelhaas

Happy

I am often glad that I received in my youth a good deal of exposure to the *King James Bible*. Although it may not be as accurate a translation as more recent versions of the Bible, it has the advantage of acquainting me with a large number of words, now obsolete, which nevertheless provide a sort of bridge to understanding what certain words mean today; for example, the word *noisome*, which is related not to *noise* but to *annoy*.

Today I have running through my mind the phrase "lest haply thou dash thy foot against a stone." Even a child can figure out that *haply*, as it is used here, does not mean "happily" or "joyfully." None (except perhaps a masochist) would be glad about smashing his foot with a rock. So what does *haply* mean here? Well, it means "by chance or luck"; it means "accidentally." "Lest accidentally thou dash thy foot against a stone." Now that makes sense.

Actually, the current meaning of the word *happy* does come from the noun *hap* meaning "luck or chance." It seems that almost from the beginning of its use, *happy* meant both "luck and good luck." Thus while it might sometimes be a synonym for joyful, it might also mean lucky or fortunate. When the *King James Bible*, translated in the seventeenth century, says of children: "Happy is the man who has his quiver full of them," it does not necessarily mean that he is whistling all day long but that he is blessed, fortunate, lucky.

That word *hap*, which we no longer use, was borrowed from the Old Norse. Our word *happen*, which also derives from it, simply means "occur." The idea of fate or chance operating is not really contained in the word *happen* the way it is in the more archaic *haply*.

Other words from that root *hap* are *haphazard*, meaning "random or unplanned" and *hapless*, meaning "luckless."

We might think of happiness as a somewhat ordinary quality—certainly something less profound than joy. But the concept of hap, that is, of blind chance, is profound and frightening. The great late-Victorian novelist and poet, Thomas Hardy, has a poem titled "Hap" which is one of the bleakest poems in the English language. Having lost all belief in any kind of God, any sense of providence, Hardy says in this poem that if he could believe that some vengeful God who found ecstasy by making him miserable caused his suffering, then he could bear the suffering. But believing as he does that the universe is entirely indifferent, that whether he experiences joy or sorrow is purely a matter of chance (hap), he is driven to despair. The real horror for Hardy is that "Crass Casualty" and "dicing Time" might have "as readily strewn Blisses about my pilgrimage as pain."

Harrow

I spent some time on the road the other day, and since it was late April and the weather was warm and dry, tractors and farm implements were everywhere–gearing up on farmyards, already working in the fields, and crawling along the highways. Sometimes, when I get behind a tractor pulling a disc or a harrow or some other implement, I get impatient, especially if I'm going up a long hill. I will occasionally pass on the hill in those circumstances, and, if a car is coming from the other way, that can be a harrowing experience.

You may have noticed that I used the word *harrow* twice in the previous sentence: Once to designate a farm implement and once to describe a frightening experience. The harrow the farmer uses is a frame with spikes or disks that cut or break up and level the ground to prepare it for planting. It literally stresses the ground. And that's where we get the word meaning "frightening or distressing." The machine stresses the ground, and a scary experience frightens or stresses the person who experiences it.

Let's look at *harrow* a bit more closely and also at another farm implement word.

The first syllable of *harrow* like the first syllable of *harvest* comes from a word that means "to cut or shear." *Harvest* suggests the time of the cutting or picking of the crop. At one time the two words might have had similar meanings, for this idea of harvesting is retained in *harrow* when it is used in traditional Catholic theology to describe Christ's descent into hell. His descent is sometimes called "the harrowing of hell" because it refers to Christ's bringing salvation to the souls held captive in hell since the beginning of the world. The harrowing of hell is the harvesting or garnering of the righteous from hell.

A farm machine that we will see on the roads in the fall is the *com*bine. I once asked a farm boy why it was called a *com*bine. "Well," he said, "because that's its name." He was unaware that the machine was so named because it com*bined* tasks that several machines–or people in the case of shocking oats–had done in earlier times. And so it came to be called a *com*bine. By now you will have realized that we have in our language a noun, *com*bine, that accents the first syllable, and when that *com*bine performs its tasks and is "verbed," we also accent the first syllable of the word. We *com*-bine oats. But any other time we use the verb we put the accent on the second syllable, we com*bine* business with pleasure.

In this piece I have com*bined harrow* and *combine*, the one word having a history that goes back a thousand years, and the other—when applied to the farm implement—just a few decades. It would be impossible to talk if we were constantly stopping to be surprised at the stories the words told. Still, it doesn't hurt for us to stop once in a while to appreciate the journeys these words have taken through the years.

Hoard

Near my home town lived an elderly farm couple who hoarded just about everything they had ever purchased or received—every grocery bag and can and box and article of clothing that they had ever had. And string! Enough to wrap the world with. When they died, my uncle bought their farm. The house was packed solid from floor to ceiling with stuff so that the only way to get through the house was through narrow trails that wound through the stuff. What a pathetic story of lives devoted to laying up worthless treasures on earth. They hoarded the cheap junk of their daily lives, and I have told their story to introduce our word for today, *hoard*.

As a noun, a *hoard* is a supply, stored up and hidden in reserve. You can hoard stuff, or, as the miser Silas Marner, you can hoard gold. *Hoard* comes from a word that means "hide" and probably referred at one time to the animal hide that might be used to cover something valuable.

But there's also a peculiarly British way of using *hoard*. In a fine essay called "Good Work and Good Works," C. S. Lewis writes this sentence: "I often see a hoarding which bears a notice to the effect that thousands look at this space and your firm ought to hire it for an advertisement of its wares." Now from the context of that sentence I can figure out what this use of hoarding means. It must be a billboard. I check my dictionary and, sure enough, that's what it is. (Incidentally, most new words we learn, not by looking them up in the dictionary, but by hearing or reading them in context and figuring out the meaning from the context.)

This *hoarding* has no etymological connection to the first one even though they are spelled the same. It means, literally, "fence" and still can be used to refer to the temporary wooden fence that is placed around a building site. On these fences, advertisements were pasted, and so eventually a

51

hoarding—at least in British usage—became a billboard. Interestingly, the word *hurdle* comes from the same source. At one time a hurdle was a portable fence used as a pen or sheepfold. From this, of course, came our word *hurdle*, a portable fence over which runners jump. This meaning of *hurdle* as an impediment to leap in a race is rather recent, first used in 1833, whereas the use of *hurdle* as a fence goes back at least to the year 1000. And now, of course, a hurdle has become an obstacle, a difficulty to be overcome, a problem to be surmounted. That meaning is really a metaphoric one and probably our most frequent use today. Yet it is so recent that the *Oxford English Dictionary* does not even list it.

What history we find in words. The little fences that my daughter jumped for four years as a high school hurdler could have been called barricades or little fences. But they are called *hurdles* because way back in 1833 people ran races that involved jumping fences, and these fences were woven-reed portable fences called hurdles borrowed from sheep farmers who used them to create movable pens. Is there a hurdler alive today who realizes that when she runs hurdles, she is linked, however tenuously, to some British sheepherder of a thousand years ago? I hope so; it's a marvelous connection.

Host

"And suddenly there was with the angel a multitude of the heavenly host praising God, and saying, Glory to God in the highest, and on earth peace, good will toward men."

What a dramatic scene! Those shepherds must have been scared out of their sandals. "A multitude of the heavenly host!" I've heard those words every Christmas since I was a kindergartener, but they can still bring shivers to my neck. As I look at them now, however, it strikes me that there's a redundancy in the text. A *multitude* is "a whole lot" and so is a *host*. So we have a host of host. But a *host* is also an army, and *host* here, according to a Greek-English lexicon I checked, means soldiers or army. A heavenly army.

To explain more fully, let me go back to the word's roots. According to John Ayto, "The Indo-European *ghostis* denoted 'stranger.' From it were descended Germanic *gastiz* (source of English *guest*), Greek *xenos* (source of English *xenophobia*), and Latin *hostis* (source of *stranger, enemy*)." So at its roots, the word *host* meant "stranger, guest, other, enemy." The negative meanings of our words *hostile* and *hostage* retain the idea of enemy. And since an invading army was made up of strangers who were enemies, *host* came to be a synonym for *army*.

But eventually, since armies are made of large numbers of people, *host* was used to signify large numbers. (Today we say, "He has a host of problems to deal with.") Using the word in both of these ways, we might transcribe the Luke 2 passage as "a host of heavenly host," a large number of heavenly armies.

Another Latin noun that probably derived from *hostis* is *hospes*. From it we have words such as *hospital, hospitality, hotel,* and *host,* meaning "one who entertains guests at home."

So there they are, three meanings of the word *host* explained: the army, the many, and the one who receives guests.

But there's a fourth meaning related to this last one: the wafer or bread of the Roman Catholic Holy Communion is called the host. The reason seems obvious and is connected to the Catholic doctrine of transubstantiation: this bread functions as the receiver of Christ as he takes residence in it. So in the same way that I host a guest who spends the night at my house, the bread hosts the living Christ.

What a lot of "hosting" was going on that first Christmas day: The angel host sang, the host of the inn had such a host of guests that he had to send Joseph and Mary to the stable, and the manger was host to the child who, at least in Roman Catholic theology, would one day take temporary residence in wafers called hosts and eaten by his followers.

Humor

Contemporary culture cannot tolerate someone who is without a sense of humor. You can be guilty of adultery or theft or lying; you can get drunk, gossip, or preen in vanity before the mirror, and people will forgive you. But if you don't have a sense of humor, if you don't laugh or even smile at a bawdy joke, a clever pun, or a pie in the face, you're in trouble. "I just don't trust the man. He's got no sense of humor."

Odd, isn't it, that we make such a to-do about a sense of humor. Certainly historic Christianity did not hold up "a sense of humor" as one of the cardinal virtues. And St. Paul nowhere suggests that "a sense of humor" is one of the fruits of the Spirit. Jesus, we read, wept; we do not read that he laughed. Sarah's laughter in the tent was the mocking sound of disbelief. And James associates laughter with worldliness.

Oh, I know an argument can be made that Jesus had a sense of humor when he told us to get the log out of our eyes before we criticized the sliver in our brother's. We say that God must have had a sense of humor when we look at the giraffe or platypus. And Elijah egging on the priests of Baal uses delicious sarcasm. God sits in the heavens and laughs at the follies of sinful humans, and the Preacher of Ecclesiastes tells us there is a time to laugh as well as weep, but he also says that sorrow is better than laughter.

Still, the Bible pays precious little attention to humor and laughter, things valued so highly in this present age. I have a hunch that we value humor so highly because as a culture we are so sad, so grim, that we seek relief in laughter. A more contented culture might not feel the need of a sense of humor so desperately. But that's just a hunch. What I know is this: The word *humor* comes from a word that means "liquid."

You knew that, of course. The aqueous and vitreous humor in the eye, for example—we know about that. Perhaps we even know about the four humors (or body liquids) of medieval medicine: bile, phlegm, choler, and blood. In medieval times it was believed that whichever of these was predominant affected one's mood. Choler made one angry or bitter; bile, that is, black bile, made one melancholy; phlegm made one dull or sluggish; and blood which gave one's complexion a ruddy glow, made one warm and cheerful.

So how did *humor* acquire its present meaning? Well, over time *humor* came to mean not the liquid but the mood or attitude indicated by the particular liquid that was dominant. Thus we still speak of someone being in a vile humor, and we mean vile mood or attitude. But eventually the word narrowed in meaning even more to indicate just one kind of mood, a funny one. So today humor does not usually mean "mood or attitude or whim," but "funniness." And if you don't have a sense of funniness, you are in trouble.

By the way, you have noticed that when a flock of geese flies south in a V, the one side of the V is always longer than the other. You want to know why? It's because there are more geese on that side.

What? You don't think that's funny? You just don't have a sense of humor.

Husband

If you are married and if you are a man, then you are a husband. But that was not always so in the English language. Until the thirteenth century, a male spouse was called a *wer*. So a married couple was *wer* and *wif*. Using *wer* as a designation of maleness has been retained, as far as I know, only in the word *werewolf*.

By the thirteenth century, the word *husband* had come into use. *Husband* is a combination of two words: *hus*, meaning "house" and *bondi*, meaning "dweller." So we have "house dweller." But early on *husband* also meant "master of a household," someone of sufficient means to own his house.

There is another meaning for *husband* as well, perhaps several. We still speak of animal husbandry, and my dictionary defines *husbandry* as "the careful management of domestic resources." Is this meaning of *husband* related to the male spouse who is a house dweller? It is, and the connection is really quite clear. If one dwells in a place, then he takes care of or manages that place. If he does this well, he is a good husband. Eventually *husband* came to mean not just caretaker but "one who manages well, carefully, frugally." Husbandry is good management. The English poet and playwright Oliver Goldsmith has this to say about Dutch people, pleasure, and husbandry: "The Dutch frugally husband out their pleasure." He may be right.

If one managed a place in the thirteenth century, it quite likely was a farm or a manor. The management of rural places involved animals and land; thus Roger Ascham says in 1545, "A good ground, well-husbanded, bringeth forth great plenty of big-eared corn."

Animal husbandry is the careful nurture and care of animals. A Scottish paper says that the chief branch of husbandry is the rearing of sheep. *Husband* meaning "animal care" and *husband* meaning "male spouse" come together in a rather strange way in the seventeenth century when the male of a pair of animals was called a husband. The bull is the husband of a cow. And the poet John Dryden says, "The bull is the husband of the herd."

William Coverdale's translation (1535) of II Chronicles 26:10 reads, "He [Uzziah] delighteth in husbandry." The NIV says, "He loved the soil." Thomas Traherne (1675) moves from literal soil husbandry to spiritual husbandry when he writes: "The heart prepared to receive it [the word] by the husbandry of providence."

So what do we have? *Husband* meaning "male spouse." That still works today. *Husbandry* as "careful and frugal management." That works but is rarely used. *Husbandry* as "the care and nurture of animals." I suppose that works today though to call a cattle confinement with thousands of steers animal husbandry would be a misuse of the word. Whether it is a misuse of animals is not yet established.

Imbecile

The morning paper's headlines scream out: "E. coli bacteria Hits Upstate New York." The bacteria are believed to have come from a well that was polluted by fecal matter from cows. E. coli is one of those aspects of modern culture that haunts us precisely because we know about it and we can't really defend ourselves against it. It may reside in the next hamburger we eat or in the next glass of water we drink. Before we knew about bacteria, in other words, before magnifying lenses existed, deaths by E. coli would have been unexplained or explained incorrectly. But now we know.

When bacteria were discovered not too long ago, they needed a name. The word *bacteria* is a diminutive of the Greek *baktron*, a staff. The word *bacillus* from the same root refers to "any of a genus of rod-shaped bacteria that occur in chains, produce spores, and are active only in the presence of oxygen." The key words here are, of course, *rod-shaped* and *staff*. *Bacteria* and *bacillus* were the words chosen to name this microscopic life form because of its stick-like appearance. (Despite this name, there are, apparently, bacteria that are not stick-like.)

The connection in sound between *bacillus* and *imbecile* is apparent even while the connection in meaning seems quite mysterious. *Imbecile* means, literally, without a staff to lean on, weak or feeble. And from this physical weakness the meaning moved to "weak or feeble in mind."

Another word meaning "a person of feeble mind" is the word *idiot*. Its meaning in both Greek and Latin was "personal" and "private." Among the ancient Greeks it was a serious and important honor to hold public office. Anyone who did not hold civil office but simply sought his own personal wealth and well-being was called *idios*. A similar usage existed later among the Romans. Their word *idiota* was applied to anyone who held no office, and it carried with it the connotation that such a person was incapable and therefore stupid.

Eventually *idiota* passed to the French and then to the English. But it did not immediately mean a person of low mental ability in English. At first an idiot was a layperson, a person without learning. Jeremy Taylor writes of "The holy and innocent idiot and plain, easy people of the Laity." These were not stupid people but uneducated. Soon, however, the current meaning came into practice. Milton writes, "By the civil law, a foole or Idiot born shall lose the lands whereto he is born because he is not able to use them aright." It is clear that the connotative meaning of *idiot* has taken quite a plunge with its present meaning of someone with little mental ability.

Thinking back to the Greek and Roman use of *idiot*, I wonder what people from those early cultures would think of American culture's emphasis on individualism and its innate distrust of almost anything associated with government. In American culture, often, those regarded as *idiota* are more likely to be engaged in public service, and the most admired are those in private enterprise.

Will the real idiots please stand up?

Inkling

Perhaps from time to time as you listened to a sermon or a lecture or the natterings of junior high adolescents, you have looked at your spouse and asked, "What are they saying?" and your spouse has replied, "I haven't an inkling." In other words, "I don't have a hint" or "I don't have a clue" what these kids are saying.

That raises for us the question: What is an *inkling*? I know that one of the most famous clubs in literary history was called "The Inklings." One of its members was J. R. R. Tolkien, author of the immensely popular fantasy trilogy *The Lord of the Rings*. This great story came about, at least in part, because of Tolkien's membership in "The Inklings," for the members of the club, which also included C. S. Lewis and Charles Williams, read their writings to one another and criticized and challenged each other.

Why did they call their club "The Inklings"? The answer always seemed obvious to me: These men—and later also a woman, when Dorothy Sayers was allowed to join the club—called themselves "inklings" because as writers they were ink-spattered, ink-smeared. They wrote before the days of computers or even ballpoint pens and therefore were most likely spattered with ink at the end of an evening of writing. So they combined the word *ink* with the suffix *ling* to create their club name. The *ling* suffix appears in other English words (*yearling, hireling, starling, sapling*) and means "a person or thing belonging to or concerned with a larger entity." Thus, a yearling is an animal that belongs to that group of animals that are a year old. Tolkien used the *ling* suffix in his nickname for his hobbits, calling these short creatures *halflings*—meaning, I'm sure, creatures who belong to that group who are half as tall as ordinary humans.

The Inkling Club members, then, designated themselves as "little old ink-spatterers."

But these writers loved words and knew their histories: Tolkien's specialization was in early Scandinavian and Anglo-Saxon languages, and another member of the club, Owen Barfield, was a linguist. So, in choosing the name of their club they must also have been aware of this other word, not having to do with *ink*, but rather meaning to hint at, to intimate, and, most literally, "to whisper." Yes, literally an *inkling* is a whisper and at one time there was a verb, *to inkle*, which meant to whisper. (As recently as 1904, novelist Thomas Hardy used the word *inkle* as a verb.)

How does this meaning apply to the club? Well, we can be sure that it is not because they conducted their meetings in hushed voices and whispers. All reports of the meetings indicate that they were loud, boisterous, full of laughing and shouting, and ale-drinking. I suppose one could argue that they were thus being ironic in using the name *inkling*–since the tone of the meeting was so much the opposite of whisperings.

But I would rather suggest that perhaps as creative artists they believed that their works–stories and poems–would *inkle*, that is, whisper or hint at some truths about human existence, about the relationship between God and humankind. Great art often works by indirection, by allusiveness, by giving readers just an inkling of God's truth.

Art inkles.

Jealous

Jealous and *zealous* are two such different words, yet–would you believe it–they come from the same source. The Greek word *zelos* denoted "jealousy as well as fervor and enthusiasm." And though *jealous* is usually considered a negative word, the use of it to describe the Lord God who punishes the children for the sin of the fathers to the third and fourth generation is not entirely negative. Rather it shows us a God who loves his children so fervently, so zealously, that he is filled with righteous indignation at their unfaithfulness.

I suppose the difference between God's jealousy and our frail human jealousy is that, very often, human jealousy, though it grows out of love, grows out of distrust as well. Often our jealousy is not based on evidence, but on ignorance, innuendo, or hearsay. Distrust seems to be at the very heart of our jealousy. As Emilia says in Shakespeare's *Othello*: "Jealous souls … are not ever jealous for the cause,/ But jealous [because] they're jealous. It is a monster/ begot upon itself."

This distrust may be the connection to the French word *jalousie*, which in the nineteenth century came from our English *jealousy* to mean "blind or shutter." The underlying sense of this word seems to be that one can look through the shutter slats without being seen. You can sense the distrust, the spying, suggested by this French meaning.

Finally, we English speakers borrowed back from the French, taking their word *jalousie*, meaning "a blind or shutter," and making it our own. So today you can go to the lumberyard or hardware store and order a jalousie window or door—one that is formed of overlapping louvers or slats that can be adjusted to regulate the air or light or spying eyes coming between them.

You may have noted that I have said nothing about *zealous*. That's because there's nothing to say. It means exactly what it meant when we borrowed the word from the Greeks: "fervor, passion." But it is a positive emotion—when it is focused on a good thing. Psalm 69:9 says, "Zeal for the house of the Lord doth eat me up." Perhaps you have known a pastor who might have said that.

Kowtow

My grandson Carter is a towheaded two-year-old who frequently has a bump or two on his forehead and grin on his face. He throws himself with a pure and reckless delight into whatever he is doing—running, climbing, dancing, wrestling, exploring. But in his reckless play he often falls—down steps, off stools and tables, on sidewalks—hence the bumps.

Carter does not get his head bumps by kowtowing. *Kowtow* is a word the English have appropriated from the Mandarin Chinese. It comes from two Chinese words, *ke*, meaning "knock or bump," and *tou*, meaning "head." The prescribed form of showing respect for important Chinese people, especially emperors, was to lie flat on one's stomach and touch one's forehead to the floor.

Eventually, *kowtow* was used in English, but usually in a metaphorical sense. Benjamin Disraeli in his novel *Vivian Grey* (1826) gives the first recorded example of this metaphorical usage: "The Marquess kotooed like a first-rate Mandarin, and vowed 'that her will was his conduct.'" We kowtow to someone when we behave in a servile or obsequious manner, when we act humble with the intent of earning favor or gaining status. In other words, *kowtowing* is usually done to persons in power positions, and it is demeaning behavior.

When my grandson Carter kowtows ("bumps head"), however, he exhibits no servile behavior and is totally uninterested in currying favor. Carter kowtows accidentally as he explores the world in pursuit of knowledge and delight.

I called Carter a towhead in my first sentence, and by that I indicated that he is a blond. I chose the word because I wondered if a connection existed between the *tow* of *towhead* and the *tow* of *kowtow*, and I have discovered that they are unrelated. Common sense could have told me as much; since the *tow* of *kowtow* means head, *towhead* would mean "headhead," an absurdity.

Rather, the *tow* of *towhead* refers to "the fiber of flax, hemp, or jute prepared for spinning by whipping or lashing it." Apparently this fiber was white or gold, and, therefore, we call white or golden-haired children *towheads*.

A final thought on *kowtow*. The redeemed of the Lord—as depicted in the Book of Revelation—do not kowtow in the metaphorical sense. Most of the time they stand and sing praises in the presence of the Father and the Lamb. But from time to time they are so overwhelmed by the majesty of God that they instinctively fall on their faces in his presence. They physically kowtow, not out of a sense of obligation or self-advancement, but out of a purely instinctive sense of the splendor of Almighty God.

Leviathan

One of my favorite Bible texts is this from Psalm 104: "There is the sea, vast and spacious, teeming with creatures beyond number ... and the leviathan which you formed to frolic there." What I love about this picture is the huge leviathan leaping and spinning out of the water, and God the Creator sitting back and watching, smiling and enjoying the show.

And I love the suggested notion that God's primary purpose in creating the leviathan was so that the leviathan could frolic in the ocean. It was not there to provide food or fuel for people; it was not there for any practical reason we can think of. It was there to frolic.

But as I read the text and think about the word *leviathan*, I become curious. When a translator reads the Hebrew word for *goat*, he/she substitutes the Greek or Latin or English word for *goat*. And so it goes with most of the translation: Parallel words and phrases replace the words and phrases from the original language. I know this is an oversimplification, but essentially that's how translation works. But what happens when there is no parallel word? *Leviathan* is a sea creature, but what kind of sea creature? We have no such creature in any European encyclopedia of fishes and mammals.

Well, apparently the scholars who translated the Greek Septuagint from the Hebrew knew what more recent archeological scholarship has revealed: That the leviathan was an image drawn from Canaanite myths, that of a monster, a coiling, gliding serpent. Since there was no creature in their experience to correspond to the leviathan, the only thing they could do is use the process of transliteration, that is, use the word that was used in the original Hebrew. Hence, *leviathan.*

We don't know for certain where that Hebrew word came from, but scholars speculate that it is from an Arabic word meaning "to twist," fitting nicely with the coiling serpent of Canaanite mythology.

Other texts in scripture give more detailed pictures of this sea monster. The entire chapter of Job 41, all 34 verses, describes the leviathan. Here is just a taste of it:

> Who dares open the doors of his mouth, ringed about with his fearsome teeth? His back has rows of shields, tightly sealed together; each is so close to the next that no air can pass between.... His snorting throws out flashes of light; his eyes are like the rays of dawn. Firebrands stream from his mouth; sparks of fire shoot out. Smoke pours from his nostrils as from a boiling pot over a fire of reeds. His breath sets coals ablaze, and flames dart from his mouth.

Clearly this is no mere whale; in fact, it sounds like a figure from European mythology, the dragon. In this passage, Jehovah God is asking Job if he can tame or catch the leviathan, and then God says, "I made him, and he does what I tell him to do." Sometimes the leviathan symbolizes evil, sometimes great power. Sometimes he is a literal, flesh and blood creature; other times he seems figurative. I'd like to believe that at one time, this creature existed—that God created such a frolicking serpent.

It seems clear, though, that *leviathan* was a word that generated fantastic images in the minds of Old Testament Israelites and filled their hearts with awe or terror.

Leviathan!

Lickety-split

Lickety-split—it flies off the tongue like spit. Someone who has never heard this word would know almost immediately what it means. Quick, tell me, lickety-split. You don't need to know the etymology, but if you are interested, it comes from that meaning of *lick* which is "a sharp blow." It's fun to say; it can't be said slowly. The squirrels outside my window careen through the giant maple lickety-split all day long.

Next, another word that speeds off the tongue (made famous, I think, by *The Sound of Music*): *flibbertigibbet*. Originally, the word was simply an onomatopoetic representation of nonsensical chatter. It still is, I suppose. A flibbertigibbet is "a chattering gossip." Even more today it is "a flighty person, one who runs from task to task without finishing anything."

Another favorite of mine is *bamboozle*. Again most of us know what it means: "To trick, sometimes by overwhelming or using force." Apparently, it comes from the Dutch *bazen, verbazen*, meaning "to astonish or stupefy." George MacDonald, the great fantasy writer, has a character say, "You wouldn't even bamboozle a little at a bazaar." In *Tattler* (a famous eighteenth century English newspaper) number 230, *bamboozle* is included in a list of words under the heading, "On the Continual Corruption of Our English Tongue." Contrary to the authors, Mr. Addison and Mr. Steele, I find *bamboozle* not a corruption but a marvelous addition to "Our English Tongue." In fact, I am flabbergasted by Mr. Addison's sentiment and will not be bamboozled by his skillful use of language.

Like most of these words today, *flabbergast* is one whose origin no one speaks about with certainty, though one source suggests that it might be a combination of *flabby* and *aghast*. That works for me since it brings to mind a picture of a person with flabby mouth wide open looking totally aghast at what has just happened. Flabbergasted. As I researched this word, I discovered a related word: *Flabbergastation*, "the state of being flabbergasted." It's a wonderful word, but it ought to refer to a place where one can go, a sort of service station, that pumps you full of high octane amazement.

Perhaps that's one thing a worship service should do–pump us full of amazement, the kind St. Paul feels when he exclaims in Romans 11:33: "Oh the depth of the riches both of the wisdom and knowledge of God! How unsearchable are his judgments and his ways past finding out!" The church as flabbergastation! Can't you just see the looks of outrage, of absolute flabbergastation, at the very thought?

Like

Slang, like the poor, we will always have with us. But that doesn't mean we have to accept it. We have the right (the duty, even, if we are English teachers) to vent our spleen from time to time about really irritating slang.

Of course it won't do any good except to make us feel better for a few minutes. But the relief one feels is reward enough.

I'm fed up with *like*. Oh, I like *like* well enough when it's used as a verb to express how one feels about something: "I like Ike" or "I like Rock music" or "I like lasagna." And I like *like* when it is used as a preposition, especially when the preposition is part of a simile. For example, "she looks like an angel" or "he smells like a skunk." I can even handle the misuse of *like* when it is used as a subordinating conjunction as in the old Winston commercial, "Winston tastes good like a cigarette should," or as in a phrase such as "like I said" which should really be "as I said."

All of this, as I have said, I can live with. What irritates me is the use of *like* as a global emphatic interjection. We have all experienced it. With the global emphatic use of *like*, instead of saying, "It's raining hard," you would say, "It's, like, raining really hard" or perhaps, "Like, it's like, raining, like, really hard."

It can even be used to give different nuances of meaning. For example, "There were *thirty* people at the party" would be rendered as "There's, like, thirty people at the party." But "there were thirty *people* at the party" would be "There's thirty, like, people at the party."

Here are few more examples: "Monica gasped, 'This is remarkable,'" would be translated as "Monica's like, 'Cool.'" Or, "I thought to myself, 'This is so weird,'" becomes "I'm like, 'This is so weird.'"

Like is also used in conjunction with the inter-phrasal inflection, usually heard in long oral narratives spoken in one continuous sentence. To give some sense of the end of a phrase, the speaker gives an upward pitch inflection every so often. I found the following paragraph in one of those comic emails forwarded to me by a friend:

> I'm like on my way to **class**, and I'm like cutting across **campus** on the **sidewalk** and **whatever**, and this guy like starts yelling at **me**, and he's all, like, "Why don't you, like ride on the **road**," and **whatever**, and I go like "there's nobody on the **sidewalk**," and **stuff**, and he's like a real **jerk**, and goes, "Bikes are supposed to stay on the **road**," and so I'm like, I'm all, okay, so this guy wants to be a jerk and **whatever**, and I'm like really late for **class**, and **stuff**, so I'm like cutting across the **lawn**....

"We were born to use words like wings," says Annie Sullivan, Helen Keller's teacher in *The Miracle Worker*. But this kind of talk uses words like they're food particles stuck in the teeth.

The writer of Proverbs says, "A word fitly spoken is like apples of gold in a pitcher of silver." How unfit are the excessive spoken *likes* we hear in contemporary discourse.

Angling in the English Stream

Line

Today I want to talk about the complexity and versatility—and in a sense, the simplicity—of the language as illustrated in a single word, the word *line*.

Line comes to us from the word *linen*, and linen, as we know, is a cloth made from flax. It was made thousands of years ago and is still made today. Not only was cloth and clothing made of linen, but also, rope. Woven linen in the form of a cord was called line. As far back as the year 1000 AD we see written evidence in English of the word *line* used to designate woven linen used as rope.

That meaning makes perfectly good sense. But where has this word gone in the past 1000 years? Here's where the versatility and the simplicity of the language come into play.

Let's imagine some surveyors taking their linen line and measuring out their boundaries to designate property lines. Pretty soon they are gone with their rope, but the boundary of the land is still called a line—a sort of metaphorical, invisible line marks out their property. It is these kinds of lines as well as national boundaries, perhaps, that the Psalmist refers to in Psalm 16: "The lines have fallen to me in pleasant places; yea I have a goodly heritage." Of course, he is also using *line* in a broad metaphorical sense as his lot in life.

But *line* does not stop there. Let me just list some other *lines* that have derived from this linen thread or cord: the assembly line, the bus line, a picket line, a telephone line, a checkout line, a line of print on a page. We say "drop me a line" when we want a letter. (And then we "read between the lines" as we try to figure out what our correspondent is really feeling or saying.) We say "toe the line" when we want someone to behave. (Or, for the same purpose, we say, "don't step out of line or you're in trouble.") We say "what's your line" if we want to know someone's occupation. We say "hold the line" when we want someone to stand firm. When we are blunt, we "lay it on the line." And if you don't believe me, you think I'm "stringing you a line."

We have fortune tellers who look at life lines, businesses devoted to bottom lines, politicians adhering to party lines, minorities segregated by color lines. We take the line of least resistance and we follow a line of reasoning.

All these different *lines* fill our talk and our writing, but do any of us native speakers say, "Well, now, just a minute. What do you mean by *line* there? I thought *line* meant boundary. I thought *line* meant linen cord. I thought it meant a row of people." No. This is what I mean by the tremendous versatility and yet simplicity of the language. We take this one four-letter word and make fifty different meanings from it, most of them metaphoric, yet nobody asks a question. It all makes perfectly good sense.

As far as I'm concerned, the lines have fallen unto me in pleasant places—not only as far as my property and national boundaries are concerned—but also in the very language I speak. Yea, I have a goodly heritage.

Magi

Why do we call the three wise men who followed the Christ star to Bethlehem, *Magi*? I thought perhaps the King James version of the Bible used the word, but no, the earliest translation that calls the wise men *Magi* is the much more recent American Standard Version. And the NIV also uses *Magi*. The King James Version calls them wise men from the east as do the earlier English translations by Caxton and Langland.

Why would a modern translation like the NIV use the less familiar word Magi? I don't know for sure, but I suspect it is because the Greek New Testament uses Magi.

Magus, the singular of *magi*, is a word of Persian origin that meant "sorcerer" and "astrologer" among other things, and I suppose it is the astrologer sense of the word that led to its use in the Greek of Matthew. In Acts, where Simon Magus appears, we get the evil sorcerer concept. That use leads us to *magic*, the other common word in our language that derives from this root. *Magic* and *Magi* are two clearly related but quite different words from this one source. Magic, especially black magic, is an avowed enemy of Christ and the church, but these Magi, these wise men from the east who proclaim a new King has been born, they are the friends of Christ and his church.

One of the great Christmas poems in the English language, written by T. S. Eliot, is titled "The Journey of the Magi." The speaker is one of the Magi, old now, looking back over his life and especially that one central event of his life, the journey to Bethlehem. The first part of the poem describes the difficulty of the journey, but then the poem concludes with a discussion of Christ's birth, being born again, the dying of our old nature, and longing for heaven:

> All this was a long time ago, I remember,
> And I would do it again, but set down
> This set down
> This: were we led all that way for

> Birth or Death? There was a Birth, certainly,
> We had evidence and no doubt. I had seen birth and death,
> But had thought they were different; this Birth was
> Hard and bitter agony for us, like Death, our death.
> We returned to our places, these Kingdoms,
> But no longer at ease here, in the old dispensation,
> With an alien people clutching their gods.
> I should be glad for another death.

The old speaker here, one of the magi, seems aware of what C. S. Lewis called deep magic, the miracle by which God used the death and resurrection of that star-found child to make all things new.

Man

A while back I accidentally heard one student talking to another. They couldn't see me and I could not see them, so I was inadvertently eavesdropping. They had just been to a college chapel service, and one of them said something like this: "I just can't believe the stupidity of our denomination. And there's no better example of it than that new hymnal they have put together." The young man's gripe was with the changes made in the words of the Christmas anthem "Good Christian Friends Rejoice." "Everybody knows," said the young man, "that when the song was written the words were 'Good Christian *Men* Rejoice.' But some feminist busybodies got a hold of it and changed the words and changed the meaning, and it makes me so mad I'm not going to chapel anymore."

Now I am sure that changes in some of the texts in the revised hymnal trip up many who sing from it now and then. And we probably all can name a particular song that we think was nearly ruined by the changes made in the text. But this young man's gripe was that the meaning of the song had been changed from what the songwriter had originally intended–the language had been made more inclusive, or so he thought.

But the young man was wrong, and he was wrong because he had a limited concept of language. He did not understand that words undergo semantic shifts that cause their meanings to change. These shifts usually occur in one of four ways: the meaning can shift from a specific thing to something more general; from something general to something more specific; from a connotation that is more negative than it once was; or to a more positive connotation than it once had. With the word *man*, the shift has been from a general meaning to a more specific meaning.

When the hymn writer wrote the word *men* in the sixteenth century, the commonly accepted meaning of the word *man* or *men* was "human being or person." In 1597, J. King writes in *On Jonas*, "The Lord had but one pair of men in paradise." Of course he is referring to Adam and Eve. Since that time the word has experienced a gradual semantic shift to something more specific, namely a male human person. If the young man had known that history, he would have realized that the word *friends*, which includes both genders, is closer to the meaning of the original than *man* is today. After all, for most of us, the primary meaning for *man* is "male person," and even though we know that mankind can mean both genders, that is not the first meaning that comes to mind when we hear the word *man*. In Old English, the sexes were usually distinguished by *wer* for man (which survives in our word *werewolf*) and *wif*, which is, of course, the source of our word *wife*. The word *woman* originated in English as a compound of *wif* and *man*. So literally it meant female person. Some feminists have gone to the opposite extreme of the student referred to earlier as they refuse to spell *woman* with an "a" in the last syllable, substituting a "y" to avoid all connection with man.

Words can be as slippery as minnows. No matter how we try to squeeze them into our hands and make them stay put, they refuse. In my own short life I have seen a number of words dramatically shift in meaning. Seen over centuries, almost all words undergo some change in meaning. The young "man" whom I overheard needs to go back to chapel, but he also should go back to the classroom, perhaps an English classroom, to learn more about his language.

Maudlin

One of the Bible characters associated with the resurrection of Christ on Easter Sunday is Mary Magdalene. It was she, you remember, who first spotted Christ in the garden and thought him the gardener until he said to her, "Mary." Then instantly she knew him. She is called Mary Magdalena because she was from Magdala near the Sea of Galilee. For centuries, European painters showed her with tear-filled eyes, crying over the death of her Lord.

In England the name Magdalen gradually slid or was condensed into the pronunciation, *maudlin*. *Maudlin* means "excessively emotional, especially, weepy." A person who cried at the drop of a hat or a harsh word from his love was said to be maudlin, overly sentimental. By now you can see that

that meaning derived from the early pictures of Mary Magdalen with tears in her eyes.

We have another English word that went through a similar sort of slide and has come to mean something quite different from the original. (Actually, quite a few British pronunciations choke out some syllables that we keep here in the States; think of words like *secretary*, *dictionary*, and *laboratory* that a Brit would pronounce as *secretry*, *dictionry*, and *laboratry*.) The word similar to *maudlin* is *bedlam*, which means, "chaos, noise, confusion." We might experience it, occasionally, in a classroom or a chicken coop. The word *bedlam*, like *maudlin*, comes from a biblical word that is pronounced quite differently, the word *Bethlehem*. How, you may be wondering, did the word *Bethlehem* come to mean "confusion"? Well, in London in the 1700s there was an insane asylum called St. Mary's of Bethlehem. This asylum was a place of confusion—people screaming and crying and behaving violently. And so gradually, the person on the street began to use the shortened form of the hospital's name, *Bedlam*, to describe any scene of noise and confusion.

Maudlin and *bedlam*, two common words derived from biblical proper nouns, and each with a meaning different from the original proper nouns: Isn't language a marvel, the way it—with a little help from its native speakers—keeps on inventing itself?

Mean

Ten-year-olds have an abruptness and an honesty about them that refreshes. We were singing that Christmas carol that goes: "All meanly wrapped in swaddling clothes and in a manger laid," when she stopped, looked up at me in the middle of the song and said, "What does *meanly* mean?" Well, I was glad she hadn't asked what *swaddling* meant. *Meanly* I could handle.

"It means," I said, "'poorly, badly, not very nicely' wrapped. In other words, they didn't have nice blankets and baby clothes."

"Well, why did they use the word *meanly*?" she asked.

I did not have a quick answer for that question, but here is my answer, a few months later. There are three distinct English words for *mean*, and each has a separate origin and history. When we say words or things have meaning, that they signify, we are using a word that comes from the Old English, *maenan*, and it is the oldest of the "mean" words.

The adjective *mean*, meaning "average, intermediate," is a derivative of the Latin *medius*, meaning "middle."

Thirdly, the word used in the Christmas carol comes from the Germanic *gaimainiz*, which means "common or shared." I have talked before about words making semantic shifts, and this is one that has had a falling connotation, a shift downward. What originally simply meant "common" or "ordinary" came gradually to mean "petty, stingy, low, ignoble, inferior." When children speak of someone as being mean, they usually mean that the person is hurtful, not nice, and this meaning comes from the same source as the *mean* in "meanly wrapped."

Using "meanly wrapped" to describe the Christ child helps to convey the humiliation of Christ from the very moment of birth: This King was dressed in very inferior garb.

The words of the sixteenth century poet Robert Southwell describe the babe of Bethlehem in language similar to that of the Christmas carol:

> This stable is his court,
> This crib his State;
> The beasts are parcel of his pomp,
> This dish his plate.
> The persons poor his liveries wear;
> The Prince is come from heaven
> This pomp is prized there.

Southwell's Baby Jesus rules in a stable, surrounded by beasts. The uniforms of his servants are the threadbare garments of the poor. This is the pomp of the Prince of Peace.

But in the end, all who have put their faith in Christ are not meanly wrapped but rather clothed in his righteousness, the very best kind of clothing to wear.

Mother

The words *father* and *mother* come from similar roots, and the roots come from the sounds an infant child makes before the child can talk. *Papa, daddy, mama, ma, mom,* and the variations in many different languages all seem to have been derived from the sounds that babies make.

The word *mother*, as far as we know, is derived from the sound a child makes while nursing or suckling at the mother's breast. Hence *mammal*–from the same root word as *mother*–is our word for "any warm-blooded animal whose offspring are fed with milk secreted by female mammary [there's that root again] glands." Obviously, *Father* does not have a similar association; it is simply a word coined to mirror a sound the child makes.

So these two words, *mother* and *father*, derive, really, from the vivid imaginations of parents interpreting the sounds of their pre-articulate children. Usually, we think of *mother* and *father* as nouns, *mother* being the female childbearer and nurturer, and *father* being the male who has begotten the child.

Now I probably have not told you anything you did not know–yet. But when we use *mother* and *father* as verbs, we–or at least I–learn something new. I learned it from friends, a mother and father, who were talking recently. The mother said to her husband that she needed to be careful that she didn't *mother* her adult children too much. By that she meant that she didn't want to advise, prod, or watch out for them too much. Her husband then said, "Well, that's okay; you can mother them, you're their mother." And she replied, "Well, why don't you father them?"

Bingo! The father tells me that he wisely kept quiet at that point, but the dialogue did teach him (and me) something about the difference between *mother* and *father* when they are used as verbs. When a woman mothers, she cares for, nurtures. When a man fathers, he impregnates. (Jacob fathered twelve sons.) To mother is "to nurture"; to father is "to sire." Ah, what language can teach about gender.

The prophet Isaiah brings together two related qualities of mothers, their nursing and nurturing, when in Chapter 66 he compares Jerusalem to a nursing mother and then compares God to a nurturing mother:

> For thus saith the Lord, Behold I will extend peace to her like a river, and the glory of the Gentiles like a flowing stream: then shall ye suck, ye shall be borne upon her sides, and be dandled upon her knees. As one whom his mother comforteth, so will I comfort you; and you shall be comforted in Jerusalem.

Narrow

One of the delightful characteristics of Emily Dickinson's poetry is her fresh and unusual use of ordinary words. She writes of *comprehending* a nectar rather than the more typical tasting of it. She speaks of *small* behavior. And, to introduce our word for today, she uses the word *narrow* in a number of interesting combinations.

In one of her poems she writes, "The narrow wind complains all day." Almost immediately it suggests to us the whining sound of a winter wind coming through a crack in a door or window or around the corner of a house. It is just the right word.

But then in another poem, "The Last Night," she uses *narrow* in quite a different context. The poem deals with the death of a young girl and the thoughts and feelings of the watchers at her bedside. In stanza four we read, "We waited while she passed;/It was a narrow time...." The connotations of this use of *narrow* are not quite so obvious. Not until I looked up the word *narrow* in the *Oxford English Dictionary* did I perhaps understood all of its connotations.

Of course on one level it might simply mean that those waiting for their loved one to die felt constricted, hemmed in, squeezed as if in a narrow physical space. But note what added significance the word has when we realize that the word *narrow* comes from a prehistoric Germanic word *narwaz* whose only modern representative is the Dutch *naar* meaning "sad" or "unpleasant." Certainly that meaning fits with a poem about a dying girl.

A further possible suggested root of *narrow* is the Latin word *nervus*, which means sinew or bowstring, and carries with it the sense of tension, tautness. This interpretation also gives meaning to Dickinson's description: a narrow time would be a tense time.

One of the metaphors for the grave that appears occasionally in English letters is the phrase "The narrow house." And the King James translation of Isaiah 28:20 contains a wonderfully vivid metaphoric use of *narrow* as it describes how the Lord will scourge the foreign rulers of Jerusalem. The terror the Lord visits on them will make them run for cover, but, the prophet writes, you will discover that "[your] bed is too short to stretch out on and the blanket too narrow to wrap around you."

Narrow–thin, tense, sad, constricted–the poets Dickinson and Isaiah catch all of its richness.

Nave

"He calls the knaves, jacks, this boy," said Estella the wealthy young snob in Charles Dickens' *Great Expectations*, "and what coarse hands he has, and what thick boots." She is speaking of Pip, a lower class lad who had come to play cards with her. Apparently, one mark of people from the upper class was that they called the jacks, knaves. (Like Pip, I call them jacks, so I know what class I belong in.) Estella's remark reminds us that the words we use often reveal things about our economic, cultural, or geographical roots.

Knave once meant "a male child." (The German word for boy, *knabe* comes from the same root.) Then it moved to meaning "a male servant," the definition Estella and her kind intended when they called the jack the knave. Finally, it came to mean "someone of low and ignoble character," the meaning that prevails today. One can see why Estella with her strong sense of class distinction would have latched on to a language trait of Pip that, at least in her eyes, emphasized the great social gulf that lay between them.

This *knave* with a "k" has no connection to the word *nave* that means the main part or body of a church. Words like *nave*, *apse*, and *chancel* are not much used today since they come from the domain of church architecture, an area that is not central to the lives of most people these days.

But this word has an interesting history. It comes from *navis*, Latin for "ship." Other words that immediately come to mind when we think of *nave* as ship are *navy* and *navigate*. If you picture a ship with its deep V that goes beneath the water and then invert it, you can see why the main part of the church was called a *nave*. The high, V-shaped ceiling of the main part of the church or cathedral looks very much like the sharp V-shaped bottom of a ship.

The connection between *nave* as ship and *nave* as church is primarily visual, I think. But another, more symbolic connection can be made as well. Think of a ship–especially a century ago when Melville wrote *Moby Dick*–as a place where the crew is made up of all different ethnic peoples and all sorts of colorful, unsavory characters: a really motley crew. Then think of a church as a ship of fools for Christ, sinners from every tongue and nation and economic class, gossips and liars and Pharisees and murderers and, yes, even knaves.

Noel

Every Christmas you sing it: "The first noel the angels did sing was to certain poor shepherds in fields as they lay. Noel, noel, born is the King of Israel." My question is, to paraphrase Philip's to the Ethiopian eunuch, "Understandest thou what thou singest?" What does *noel* mean anyway? And while you're pondering that, ponder this: Why do we call a manger scene a nativity scene?

Well, let's start with *nativity*. The word *native* goes back to the Latin word *nasci*, meaning "to be born." So the nativity scene is quite simply the scene of birth–particularly, Christ's birth. The word *noel* comes from the same root (an earlier form being *nowel* from which the word *novel* also comes). The first noel, then, is the first birth announcement that was made by the angels.

Another familiar word from this root is the French *naive*, which means, of course, "innocent," literally, perhaps, "born yesterday."

Since we are on the subject of familiar Christmas carols, let me note an interesting little paradox in this children's carol: "Away in the manger, no crib for a bed, the little Lord Jesus lay down his sweet head" (1885). What that line says is that the baby Jesus did not have a crib for a bed. Rather, he had a manger. Here is the interesting thing about the word *crib*: In Old English the word *crib* meant "manger." Not until the seventeenth century did it develop its present meaning of a "baby's bed." So taken quite literally in seventeenth century parlance, the song would say, "Away in the manger, no manger for a bed."

Between the Old English *crib* meaning "manger" and the seventeenth century *crib* meaning "baby's bed" was another meaning, "basket." If we take the idea of the manger and the basket, and put them together, we can explain our use of the word corncrib, a farm building that has a sort of woven quality, like a basket, a place to store corn. So the meaning of *crib* seems gradually to rise in connotation, moving from manger to basket to baby's bed.

The word *crib* has contributed another word to our Christmas lexicon: *crèche*. You know what I mean: Those nativity scenes with the barn or shed that houses the key figures in the Christmas drama as well as the animals. Vulgar Latin borrowed Old High German *kripja*, changed it to *creppia*. From that, the French got *crech*. And we English and Americans borrowed the word from the French.

The English language has an ecumenical quality about it, receiving into its body contributions from almost every tongue. Sort of like the church of the One who was born in the crib, *crèche, kripja, creppia*.

Noise

I occasionally entertain or annoy my family by speculating on the relationships between words. The other day I wondered aloud whether there might be a connection between the word *noise* and the word *annoy*. In this case, when my children laughed at my connecting of these two words, they were correct; there is no connection.

I suppose the reason I connected the two has to do with my memory of a comment C. S. Lewis makes somewhere that he believes the defining characteristic of hell might be noise. I have always appreciated that observation especially in this time of hard rock music. (But now I'm displaying my prejudice, so let me instead get on with the words *noise* and *annoy*.)

Noise comes, strangely enough, from the Latin word *nausea*, which is also the source of the English word *nausea*. "The confusion and hubbub that comes when a person is sick, especially seasick," is what *nausea* originally meant. And that definition explains our contemporary meaning of *noise* as "discordant or disagreeable sounds." I suppose one of those disagreeable sounds associated with nausea and seasickness was the noise of someone vomiting. The Old French later added the idea of a dispute to the word *noise*. According to John Ayto in his *Dictionary of Word Origins*, the Modern French meaning of *noise* still carries with it the "dispute" element whereas the English noise means primarily "intrusive sound."

We read in the *King James Bible* of the "noisome pestilence" (*noisome* meaning "harmful"), but that word has no connection to *noise*. Rather it is connected to the word *annoy*. (So you see my connecting of *noise* and *annoy* was not so preposterous.)

Annoy comes from the Latin phrase, *in odio*, literally, "in hatred." Say *annoy*, and then say *in odio*. You can hear how the one came from the other. The word *annoy*, now exclusively a verb, once functioned as a noun as well, as in this quote from Shakespeare's *Richard III*: "Good angels guard thee from the boares annoy." In the French language, the Latin *in odio* eventually became *ennui*, meaning "the feeling of mental weariness and dissatisfaction produced by want of occupation, boredom." Lord Chesterfield wrote, "Living like a gentleman was dying of ennui."

So there we have it: *Noise* coming originally from the word *nausea*. *Noisome*, now archaic, coming from the Latin *in odio* along with *annoy* and *ennui* and *odious*.

And now before I annoy you or ennui sets in, let me conclude with this blessing: God keep you from all annoy.

Nostril

To be thrilled usually means to be ecstatic, overjoyed; to be really, really pleased by something. But etymologically it means "to make a hole in." In fact, the word *nostril* is literally "nose thrill, nose hole."

When I learned that *thrill* meant "to make a hole," I assumed immediately that *drill* must be from the same root. But the *Oxford English Dictionary* says, "No." The English verb and noun *drill* were probably from the Dutch and have no etymological connection with *thrill* or its roots, *thirl* and *thyrlian*.

Perhaps you are wondering, as I did, how a word that means "to make a hole" came to mean "overjoyed." It happened because of a metaphorical use of *thrill*. Instead of the literal "making a hole" the word came to be used to describe a sudden stab of emotion—of joy or anger or fear or regret—like a dagger to the heart, a hole bored to the heart. For quite a while, then, *thrill* meant any kind of strong emotion that penetrated one's heart. In fact, we still keep that meaning when we talk of a novel or movie as a "Thriller." We don't mean it is a happy book necessarily, but a book that triggers all kinds of emotions.

But primarily now, *thrill* refers only to the very positive emotion of excitement or joy. Thus we can trace a movement from a literal meaning, "to make a hole," to a metaphorical meaning, "pierced with a strong emotion," to the more limited meaning of just one emotion, "excitement."

But let's go back to the literal meaning, "to make a hole." A while back our youngest daughter, Rebecca, came home from college for the weekend with a small gem embedded in her nose. A professional piercer had made a small hole in her nose, giving her, if I speak literally, a third nostril. He then placed a gem in that hole, which was attached somehow to a corresponding back piece that was inside the nose. Neither her mother nor I was particularly pleased.

A while later we were reading in Genesis the story in which Abraham's servant journeys to the land of his family to find a wife for Abraham and Sarah's son Isaac. When the servant arrives, he sees a young woman (her name is Rebekah) taking water from the well, and the servant says to himself, "If she responds to my request for a drink by offering to water my camels also, she will be the woman for Isaac to marry." She does exactly as he hopes, offers water for the camels. The servant responds by taking out of his pack a nose ring and two bracelets. Then, he "put the ring in her *nose* and the bracelets on her arms and bowed down and worshipped the Lord" (Genesis 24:47). Well, my wife and I thought, maybe we shouldn't have made such a fuss about our Rebecca's nose gem.

But we still weren't thrilled with it.

Office

The poet Robert Hayden has a wonderful poem, "Those Winter Sundays," that shows in evocative detail the various duties a father does as part of his daily obligation to his family. He builds the fire in the morning; he polishes the Sunday shoes; he works outdoors all week in the "blueblack" cold. The poem is told from the perspective of an adult remembering his childhood and recognizing now that all those tasks his father did were done out of love, and he ends the poem with a terribly heartfelt lament:

> What did I know, what did I know
> of love's austere and lonely offices?

It's a beautiful poem, a sad poem, full of the recognition and regret that come when an adult reflects on things he took for granted as a child. When I taught this poem to high school students, I always had to spend some time glossing the word *office*. "What does the poet mean by the phrase 'love's austere and lonely offices'?" I would ask and then often receive only puzzled looks. To most students the word *office* meant simply a small cubicle or room in which someone did some sort of deskwork. Students were unfamiliar with the idea of an *office* as a position, a job, or a duty. Usually if I mentioned the office of elder or deacon, they responded with recognition. They realized that Hayden's use of *office* did not refer to some workspace but to a position with certain obligations or duties.

The word *office* is a combination of two Latin words, *opus*, meaning "work," and *facium* meaning "to do." Literally then, *office* means "to do work." As Hayden uses it in the poem, it is a noun, the tasks or jobs that are motivated by love. It is a word that has, over the years, been invested with a significance that goes well beyond the literal meaning of doing work. I imagine that almost any position, if it were perceived as an office, would be taken more seriously than if it were merely a job.

In Hayden's poem, "love's austere and lonely offices" are the many hard, demanding, and lonely duties a parent does–usually without thanks from her children–simply because parental love carries with it these duties. Only later will the children realize that in the performance of these offices the parent is loving them. Whether it is polishing the shoes or building the fire or washing the clothes or working in weather that is achingly cold or chauffeuring children to lessons and games, the parent is performing the offices of parenthood.

Perhaps even as you sit in your office working overtime, you are engaged in one of love's lonely offices. Thinking of such a duty as "love's office" might just make the work seem less austere and lonely.

David Schelhaas

Pain

Today's word is *pain*. It is a word that words cannot capture. No matter how vivid our description of pain, the description will be unable to convey the actual pain. Here, in an essay called "The Language of Pain" (1994), is Dr. Richard Selzer's attempt to describe the pain of a kidney stone:

> Whom the stone grips is transformed in one instant from man to shark; and like the shark that must remain in perpetual motion, fins and tail moving lest it sink to terrible black depths of pressure, so the harborer of stone writhes and twists, bending and unbending in ceaseless turmoil. Now he straightens, stretches his limbs, only to draw them upon his trunk the next moment and fling his body from one side to the other, finding ease in neither. From between his teeth come sounds so primitive as to trigger the skin to creep. He shudders and vomits as though to cast forth the rock that grinds within.... Seed pearls of sweat break upon his face. In a moment his hair is heavy with it. His fingers scrabble against the bed, the wall, his own flesh to tear relief from these surfaces.

And he goes on. Any of us that have experienced a kidney stone may say, "Yeah, that's the way it is." But our memory of the pain can not recreate the pain we felt when we carried the stone. Even metaphor can't capture our pains: "It felt like a boulder was on my chest," we might say, or "It feels like a lion is ripping at my throat."

The word *pain* comes from a Latin word *poena* and had as its first meaning, "punishment"; *penalty* is from the same root. We see this *penalty* meaning in the phrase "on pain of death." Chaucer writing "The Knight's Tale" uses the phrase "Up on payne of lesynge youre heed" ("Upon pain of losing your head"). That phrase says nothing about suffering, though decapitation surely hurts; the word *pain* as used here refers to the punishment of death. But the common meaning we have for *pain* today is suffering, or as the *Oxford English Dictionary* says, "the absence of pleasure"; that meaning developed toward the end of the fourteenth century. It is not hard to see how. Punishments usually involve suffering, so eventually the word for suffering becomes the primary meaning of a word that first meant "punishment." It is another example of language usage determining meaning.

A related word from the same Latin source is the word *pine*, meaning "to long for." It comes also from *penalty* meaning "punish" or more accurately here, "torture." The lover separated from her loved one pined for him, that is, she was tortured by his absence.

Some of the best words about pain come from old Saint John who writes in Revelation 21:4, "And God shall wipe away all tears from their eyes; and there shall be no more death, neither sorrow, nor crying, neither shall there be any more pain...."

Pantry

Any of us who have lived past middle age are aware of words that are gradually disappearing from everyday usage. One such word is *pantry*. I suppose it has disappeared from usage largely because modern houses seldom have pantries. We have refrigerators and freezers and special rotating shelves for cans, but seldom, pantries.

That word *pantry* is etymologically a "bread room." The *pan* part of the word is from the Latin *panis*, meaning "bread." The second half of the word is derived from the last syllable of the Old French *panetier*—"servant in charge of bread."

French composer Charles Gounod has a song, *Panis Angelicus*, which means literally, bread of the angels. Whenever I sang that song at weddings, the English translation was "Oh Lord Most Holy." It makes one wonder about the freedom Protestant translator's took with Catholic songs, for neither word, *bread* or *angel*, appears anywhere in the popular English translation.

As I searched my mind for other words that have the *panis* root in them, I thought of marzipan, that sweet almond paste used in making delicious bars and breads, especially around Christmas.

Apparently many people have assumed that *marzipan* came from a combination of the Latin *panis* and the Latin *marci*, meaning "Mark" (referring to the gospel writer). They and I were wrong. The *pan* in this word has nothing to do with bread. Instead, the word *marzipan* has a terribly convoluted history. The word originated in Arabic and meant literally "the King who sits still." This was applied by the Saracens to a medieval Venetian coin that had a figure of the seated Christ (as king) on it. Eventually, according to John Ayto, the word's meaning "progressed from the 'coin' via 'measure of weight or capacity,' to a 'box of such capacity,' and finally to 'such a box containing confectionery.'" The confectionery, of course, was that delicious almond bar.

You may be wondering whether our word *pancake* came from the Latin *panis*. The answer is "no." That *pan* came from the West German *pfanne* and Dutch *pan*, meaning "plate or dish." These words probably derive from the Latin *patina*, not the Latin *panis*.

Isn't that the way it goes. You think you have these words all figured out but when you dig a bit deeper, nothing seems to pan out.

David Schelhaas

Pavilion

In Psalm 19 the poet tell us that "in the heavens God has pitched a tent for the sun," that the sun is "like a champion running his race" and "like a bridegroom coming forth from his pavilion" (New International Version). Now perhaps when you hear the word *pavilion*, you think of a platform of some kind—I know that's the first image that comes into my head. And that is not completely wrong. One of the meanings given for *pavilion* in a standard dictionary is "part of a building jutting out from the main building, often covered like a porch."

The primary meaning of the word *pavilion*, however, is "tent." When the Psalmist uses it in Psalm 19, he is quite likely referring to the four posted-tent used in the Jewish wedding ceremony. So the word *tent* in the first part of the verse and the word *pavilion* in the second part of the text are really synonyms. God has made the sky—a tent—and the sun is like a bridegroom, glowing with pride and energy and eagerness and joy, coming out of the darkness of that tent or pavilion.

The word *pavilion* comes from the Latin word *papilo*, which means "butterfly." Apparently someone in Roman times saw a pointy-topped tent with its two "doors" spread wide open, and it reminded her of a butterfly, a *papilo*. Old French for the word was *pavilion*, and the English took the word from the French. This looking at one thing, a tent, and having it remind us of another thing, a butterfly, is really the making of metaphor. We do it all the time: The coat rack standing in the hallway becomes a hall tree. The genealogy diagram of your ancestors becomes a family tree. Someone looked at the little device next to his computer with a cord coming out of one end and said, "Mouse." Right now, as I click to italicize *mouse*, I use a mouse (and a metaphor).

As is so often the case, words begin as metaphors; this metaphoric butterfly eventually became an ordinary word in our language, and today hardly a soul thinks of butterfly when they hear the word *pavilion*. Most don't even think of a tent.

While we're on the subject of tents, let me note that the word *tent* means stretched. The early tents were animal skins stretched tight. Our word *tense*—meaning "nervous, uptight, stretched tight"—obviously comes from the same source, but with *tense*, the word is applied to our muscles or nerves being stretched tight rather than animal skins.

I see that the sun, that champion runner, has run half his race, and it is time for me to eat lunch. Perhaps, as an antidote to tension, I should take a nap as well.

Peculiar

> Let every nation rise and bring
> Peculiar honors to her king.

Many of us know these words from a stanza of the old hymn "Jesus Shall Reign Where'er the Sun." In a more recent rendition of the song, however, the word *peculiar* has been replaced and the line is now,

> Let every nation rise and bring
> Her highest honors to her king.

It is not difficult to figure out why the change was made because for most people *peculiar* means "odd" or "strange," sometimes even "weird." Why would nations want to bring strange honors to their God? Of course, many of us know that *peculiar* also means "unique," or "special," or "distinctive." Bringing honors to our God that are unique or special or distinctive makes perfectly good sense, But, most people who read or sing the word *peculiar* think of *odd* immediately, so the word does not work very well in the song. The change made by the hymnal committee was a good one, in my estimation.

But having sung the hymn in church this past Sunday, I now am curious about the roots of the word *peculiar*, and, as might be expected, I have discovered that they tell an interesting story. *Peculiar* comes from a Latin word *peculiaris*, which means of "private property," and this peculiaris derived in the Latin from the word pecus meaning "cattle" and also "wealth," since wealth was sometimes measured, by the number of cattle one owned. Our English word *pecuniary* comes from the same root as the word *peculiar.*

But how then did *peculiar* come to mean "different or strange or distinctive"? Think of it like this. My wealth is what I own by myself. It is distinctively mine and different from your wealth. It is my private property, not shared with others. Peculiar. From there it is easy to see how it split into two meanings, one having a sort of negative connotation, odd; the other a positive connotation, unique or distinctive.

So, *peculiar* once meant wealth and comes from an early word for cattle. The word *fee* has a similar history. It comes from the first syllable of the early Anglo-Norman word for *feudal*, which at one time referred to the land that was granted to someone as a reward for service. In other words, the land was a fee (or payment) for services. If *fee* is traced all the way back to its roots, it also, like *peculiar* and *pecuniary*, meant "cattle" or "cattle-property." The first syllable of our word *fellow* also comes from that word, a "fee-low" being someone who lays down money, who invests with others in a property. He is a business partner and then, by a broadening of meaning, one who shares with another in any work.

Before our more abstract concept of money developed, one's wealth was measured in things, and payment for service was given in concrete valuable stuff. Another example that comes to mind is the word *salary* which derives from the word *salt* and reminds us of a time when people received their pay in actual salt.

So it does not seem strange to me that *fee*, *pecuniary*, and *salt* all derive from concretely valuable things. It does seem a bit peculiar to me that *peculiar* also derives from one of these wealth words since it no longer has a monetary meaning. But then, words are peculiar, odd, strange–weird, even.

Peony

One of the best things about living in a Northern climate is rounding the curve that takes us from winter to spring, from cold to warm, from brown to green, from no flowers to a land lush with flowers. As we move from May to June, the whole land seems to be in bloom. Few flowers are more typical of these parts and of rural life in general than the peony. (Most of the farms gardens I have seen–my mother-in-law's in particular–have had long lines of peonies.) Every year around the second week of June, these gaudy, short-lived beauties burst on to the scene, extravagant in their fragrance. Pink and violet and purple and white–the fist-sized blossoms are as fragile as they are gaudy.

The poet Jane Kenyon calls peonies her favorite flowers, remarking that peonies "are not Protestant work-ethic flowers. They loll about in gorgeousness; they live for art; they believe in excess. They are not quite decent, to tell the truth."

Another contemporary New England poet, Mary Oliver, writes of "their honeyed heaviness, their lush trembling,/ their eagerness,/ to be wild and perfect for a moment, before they are/ nothing, forever."

The name peony comes from the Greek, *paeonia*, after Paion, another name for the Greek god Apollo who was the physician of the gods. The flower was called *peony* because it was believed for a long time to have healing properties. Sylvester writes in 1591: "About an Infants neck hang Peonie, It cures Alcydes cruel Maladie." Phillips writing in 1709 says that the peony roots have great use in physic, that is, as medicine, or perhaps, in

81

particular, as a laxative. Clearly the peony has been around for a long time and in fact might have come to us from the Romans via the English.

Phlox are also profuse right now, both as domesticated flowers in people's yards and as wild flowers blooming on the edges of rivers, woods, and ditches. The phlox I see most often are pinkish lavender, but apparently they can be white, red, and bluish as well. The word *phlox* comes from the Greek *phlegein*, meaning "to flame or burn." I can only surmise that the colorful phlox flamed out of the grasses and woods like a fire, a conflagration, occasioning the name. In 1706 Phillips writes of the phlox as a flower "of no Smell but of fine Flame-colour." (Incidentally, the word *flagrant*, which we usually use to mean "outrageous," comes from this same root and meant, "burning, glaringly bad, notorious.")

The aster is, of course, a star. *Aster* is Latin for star. Most often the asters we see are purple with a gold center. The New England Aster is one of our native prairie flowers. Actually, if you think about it, the asterisk on your typewriter or computer is shaped very much like the flower and both resemble stars as we see them from a great distance. "*Aspera astra*," the high school Latin teachers of the past used to say. "Reach for the stars." Good advice in an age and culture that rarely teaches Latin or points young people to the stars.

Pew

I attend a church that has no pews. We are pewless (which is not necessarily to say we are odorless). A few years ago we sold the wooden pews and replaced them with individual chairs that can be hooked together or stand alone. I am not going to attempt to explain why we did that, but I want to present a mystery: If we could take our present church with its individual blue chairs and move it a couple of centuries back in time, we would say it has pews.

How is that possible? Listen to the first definition of *pew* given by the *Oxford English Dictionary*: "A raised standing-place, stall, or desk in a church to enable a preacher, reader, or other officiant to be seen and heard by the congregation; often with a defining word as with minister's pew, pulpit, prayer or praying pew, reading or readers pew, a lectern...." It sounds as if the pew was not what it is today—not a place where the average parishioner sat and listened, but a place from which the preacher or reader or prayer leader led the worship. And at my church we still have two such raised places.

The word *pew* goes back, ultimately, to the Greek *podion*, which means "small foot or base." In Latin this became *podium*, which also became an English word meaning "raised place, pulpit, or balcony." The Latin *podium* became, though I can't adequately explain how, the French *peu*, meaning "hill or height." The English took this form from the French and used it to designate an elevated place where certain people sat or from which they presented.

Gradually, however, the word *pew* came to mean the opposite of pulpit or podium–the opposite of a raised place. In 1882, J. Parker asks, "How can we preach to a people unprepared to hear?–A prepared pulpit should be balanced by a prepared pew." Here *pew* is clearly a word that means the place where the ordinary parishioner sits–the opposite of the pulpit and the clergy.

Even though the *pew* or *box-pew* designated a place where worshippers sat, up until the twentieth century these pews seemed frequently to be the seats where the noble and wealthy sat. Often they were handed down from generation to generation, and people usually had to pay a rental fee to sit in them. There were even pew women to collect fees. Some pews had locks so only the owners could sit in them. They were, I suppose, indicative of the class-system that existed in Europe rather than the classless system that exists in the kingdom of God.

This class system must have been a problem from the very earliest days of the church. In the second chapter of James we read the following:

> My brothers and sisters, as believers in our glorious Lord Jesus Christ, don't show favoritism. Suppose a man comes into your meeting wearing a gold ring and fine clothes, and a poor man in shabby clothes also comes in. If you show special attention to the man wearing fine clothes and say, "Here's a good seat for you," but say to the poor man, "You stand there" or "sit on the floor by my feet," have you not discriminated among yourselves and become judges with evil thoughts?

In the churches of my youth certain pews had special significance. They had small metal plates on them that said, "Elders" or "Pastor's Family." In my church such designations are a thing of the past, and I am glad. For, while the church is not a democracy, neither is it a place where anyone needs to be singled out as more important than anyone else.

Ponder

A friend recently told me he had been pondering the word *ponder*, and he wondered in his pondering if a connection existed between *ponder* and *pond*. (I like to picture him back-floating in a pond of water, pondering as he gazed up at the clouds, but he probably did his pondering on the job or in church.) In any case, the short answer is "no"; *pond* and *ponder* are not related. Here is the longer answer.

The word *ponder* comes from the Latin *ponderare* which means to weigh. And so we weigh an idea in our mind, we consider it, we ponder it. A related adjective is *ponderous*, that is, heavy. The word *ponder*, which we use now exclusively to mean "think deeply or consider," was at one time a noun used to mean "weight." As recently as the seventeenth century, we read: "God made all thing and set it sure, In Number, Ponder, and in Measure." A translation of Ovid in 1621 contains this line: "The Rock, by its own ponder firmly fortified." Of course, the most obvious relative of the root form of *ponder* is our word *pound*, a weight of sixteen ounces.

Interestingly, a relative form of the Latin *ponderare* is the Latin *pendere* from which a number of related "weight" words have come words like *pendant* and *pendulum* with their hanging weights, but also words like *pansy* and *pensive*. *Pensive* means "reflective, thoughtful, pondering"; the pansy was thought to be a pensive flower.

The word *pond* is also related to the *pound* that we use when we refer to the dog-pound. In Middle English, *ponde* was a variant of *pound*. And the two are still used in the same sense in some Scottish and English dialects. William Coverdale's 1535 translation of Isaiah 19:10 reads, "All the poundes of Egipte, all the policie of their Moates & ditches shal come to naught." Isaiah is talking about fishponds here.

Both the pond and the pound are enclosures, the pond an artificial construct containing water and fish; the pound as it was used in England most frequently was an enclosure for the detention of stray or trespassing cattle. Today, of course, the pound houses stray and trespassing dogs and cats.

So we see here two kinds of *pounds*, one a weighty word coming from the same source as *ponder*, the other denoting an enclosure and coming from the same source as *pond*.

Here's a bit of doggerel that followed me into this pond essay:

> A fat cat from the pound
> Fell into a pond.
> He couldn't dog-paddle.
> Sadly, he drowned.

David Schelhaas

Possess

Richard Wilbur's poem, "A Summer Morning," paints a picture of a cook and a gardener who work on a large estate. The young owners of the estate, who came in late the night before and are still abed, will miss the beauty of the morning. But the cook as she breaks an egg in the morning sunlight and listens to the songs of thrush and catbird, and the gardener who savors the view of the flowers, lawn, and big house as he works his shears, both celebrate the beauty of the morning on the estate: "He and the cook alone/Receive the morning on their old estate,/Possessing what the owners can but own."

Reading a line like this—"possessing what the owners can but own"—makes one wonder about the difference between possessing and owning.

The word *possess* comes from two Latin words, *potis* and *sidere*, which mean literally "to sit down as the person in control." But it did not necessarily mean to own—especially in its early usage. The idea of sitting down in a place, inhabiting it, gets at something of what *possess* meant a few hundred years ago. Milton in *Paradise Lost* tells how man was given "Dominion ... over all other creatures that possess earth, air, and sea." The creatures don't own the earth, air, and sea, but they possess it. And John Bunyan in *Pilgrim's Progress* describes the city of destruction as a place "possessed with a very ill-conditioned and idle sort of people."

Christina Rosetti a couple of centuries later writes of bells possessing the mid-day air. We may have heard our grandmothers use *possess* in a similar way when they said, "Possess yourself of patience, young man."

At the same time, *possess* was also used as a verb that meant "to bestow upon or give." Thomas Jefferson writes in one of his letters, "I have thought it better to possess him immediately of the paper."

When we own a house or car, we are given a deed or title to it. And, of course, *possess* can be used in that context also. We possess our houses and cars and clothes and stock portfolios. A phrase such as "Possession is nine-tenths of the law" suggests that ownership and possession are exact synonyms. But as I have noted, *possess* means so much more than that.

If we look again at the gardener and cook in Wilbur's poem we see that their possessing of the old estate is more significant than the owner's owning of it. The cook and gardener sit down with power (the power of pleasure and delight) on the old estate while the owner's miss that pleasure and delight. As the creatures possess the earth, as the bells possess the air, the gardener and cook possess the beautiful morning on the grand old estate.

Earlier this year I received an e-mail from a colleague who referred to his house not as something he owned but as something over which he has been given temporary stewardship. I like that. He might also have said he *possessed* it if the older meaning of *possess* still prevailed.

Pupil

I have noted before that as the meanings of words change over time they usually change in one of two ways. One way is by rising or falling in connotation. For example, a word like *villain*, which today, of course, suggests a really evil person, once simply meant "a feudal serf, a dweller in a villa, a farm worker." The word *villain*, then, has had a descending connotation, from "farm worker" to "scoundrel." But the word *villa* has had an ascending connotation. Once it simply denoted a farm house, but today it suggests in our minds "a rather extravagant house and grounds in the country—an estate almost."

That was a quick illustration. The other way that a word's meaning changes is that it moves to a more general meaning or it moves to a more specific meaning. I want to spend a bit more time with the word *pupil* and some of its relatives to illustrate this kind of movement. The Latin root for *pupil* is *pupa*, meaning "girl," and *pupas*, meaning "boy"; these are also the roots for such words as *puppet* and *puppy*. *Puppet* is a diminutive form of *pupa* (girl) and means "doll or toy doll"; *puppy* is literally "a toy dog," and at one time it might have referred to a small dog, a lapdog, rather than necessarily a young dog.

Pupil also comes from that boy/girl root. But it did not always mean, as it does today, student. Its earlier meaning in English was "orphan." In his fourteenth century translation of the Bible into English from the Latin Vulgate, John Wycliffe translates a part of James 1:27 as follows: "visit pupilles and the widow in her tribulation." What he meant by "pupilles" is, as all subsequent English translations put it, "orphans."

The meaning of pupil as "person being taught" did not emerge until the sixteenth century. And then it was both a verb and a noun, so that Porter writes, "Have I seen thee pupell such green young things and with thy counsel tutor their wits?"

So we see how the word *pupil*, which once in English referred to a rather specific group of children, namely orphans, came to refer to all children who are taught, even those who might be in college. But we also see how it once referred to orphans in any situation but now refers only to school children. With one part of its meaning it becomes more general and the other part more specific. Funny how hard it is to make words fit into a nice, neat system.

By the way, the pupil in your eye also comes from that same Latin root meaning boy or girl and puppet and puppy. Why? If you stand very close to someone and look into her eyes you will see a little doll-like image of yourself reflected in her pupil.

Quarantine

While reading a biography called *Galileo's Daughter*, "a memoir of love, faith and science," as the subtitle says, I ran into an explanation of the word *quarantine*. Now, we all know that to quarantine someone means to isolate him, to keep him apart from any interaction with the public. What I did not know was that the word means quite literally "forty days." At one time a quarantine was a space of forty days, and people with a contagious disease or under censure by the Pope might be isolated for forty days. Today, of course, it means any period of seclusion, one day or a hundred. So we can see that the meaning of the word has broadened out, moved from being quite specific to more general.

Actually, a large number of words in our language come from numbers. With many of them we immediately recognize the number—unity, bicycle, trinity. But there are others, like *quarantine* for me, that we don't immediately recognize as words derived from numbers.

Do you, for example, see the word *one* in *unanimous*? Probably you all do. You are of one mind in that, unanimous. And what about *duplicate*? Isn't it odd that when we duplicate, literally double, we go to the duplicating machine and make not one duplicate but many? So a duplicating machine doesn't simply double but doubles and doubles and doubles.

Most of us have never seen our duodenum, the first section of our small intestine. If we did, would we see the reason it is called a duodenum? *Duodeni*, the root of *duodenum*, means "twelve," and the length of that section of the intestine is about twelve fingers' breadth.

What is a trivet? It used to be a three-legged stand on which pots or kettles could be held over a fire. Today more often it is a short-legged metal or ceramic plate for holding hot dishes on a table. It may or may not have the three legs suggested by the word *tri-vet*, three feet.

87

One, two, three—unanimous, duplicate, trivet. What about four? Well, we've already mentioned the four in *quarantine*, and we all know quart as a fourth of a gallon and quarter as a fourth of a dollar. But did you know that *quarter round*, the rounded piece of molding that may be on your floor up against the mopboard, is, in cross section, a quarter of a circle? I must confess that I had only heard the word—never seen it in print and had assumed that it was *cord around*. Talk about ignorant.

I'll conclude this little numbers game with words from both the Greek *penta* and the Latin *quin* that mean five. *Pentagon* and *quintuplet* we know quite well. What about *quintessence*?

Quintessence in ancient and medieval philosophy was "the fifth essence, or ultimate substance," of which heavenly bodies were thought to be composed: distinguished from the four elements—earth, fire, water, air. Today we often mean the most perfect manifestation of something. For example, someone might say that John Wayne was the quintessential American male; that the '57 Chevy is the quintessential American automobile; that a mother, father, son, and daughter make up the quintessential American family; that *The Godfather* is the quintessential American movie.

And the quintessential American word? *Okay*.

Rake

It's late fall, and most of the leaves have been raked or vacuumed or left to blow where they wish. But for a few weeks in late October, after the last heavy rains, a flurry of raking activity occurred all over town. As I sit here in my office during the Thanksgiving break with a foot-high stack of freshman research papers, I am reminded of a poem by Howard Nemerov called "Absent-Minded Professor." The poem describes how an old retired professor has nearly been forgotten and how his "bright replacement" stays busy

> At the desk correcting papers, nor ever grieves
> For the silly scholar of the bad old days,
> Who'd burn the papers and correct the leaves.

There's something I like about that old guy who'd burn the papers and correct the leaves. It is a beautiful day, and I would really like to grab a rake and correct the leaves left on my lawn. But instead, I'll grab that word *rake* and talk about it for a little while.

Rake, meaning "a bar with teeth fixed across it and attached to a long handle," goes back to the prehistoric German *rek* meaning "to gather or heap up." And it may go back finally to the Indo-European *rog* meaning "stretch." In this definition we see how the rake is really "an extension of the hand, a stretching out of the hand." The teeth of the rake are like fingers and the handle like an arm.

Another meaning for *rake* not often used these days is "a man of loose habits, an immoral fellow; a dissipating man of fashion." The English playwright Richard Brinsley Sheridan writes of "a dissipated rake who has squandered his patrimony." This *rake* is a shortened form of the word *rakehell*, and the meaning of that word comes from the idea that one would have to rake through hell to find someone quite as bad as this fellow, this rakehell, this rake.

Another meaning of *rake* from another source altogether is "slant or inclination." We speak of a floor in a theater or church as being raked, slanted. When we speak sometimes of a hat being worn at a rakish angle, it is this meaning we have in mind, though it might very well be a rake, a dissolute fellow, who wears his hat at such an angle.

But I am interested in the rake as tool, a tool to get us desk-bound folk out of the office and into God's good creation.

Rape

When I taught high school, one of the standard works in the English Literature anthologies that I used was an excerpt from Alexander Pope's long poem, *The Rape of the Lock*. It is one of the best known and most highly regarded literary works of the eighteenth century, a social satire which describes in cunning and satiric detail a young man's plan to snip a lock of hair from the head of the beautiful Belinda as a love token. Pope uses the word *rape* because the primary meaning of *rape* in the eighteenth century was "the act of taking anything by force." It comes from the Latin *rapere*, meaning "to seize or take."

Interestingly, *rapere* is also the source of the word *rapture*. We often use this word to describe the time when Christ returns to earth to (depending on your theological interpretation) take the redeemed to heaven or cast the

89

unredeemed into utter darkness. In either case, the meaning "to seize or take" is clearly evident in the rapture.

But almost all native speakers of English today would insist the word *rape* means "the sexual violation of another person, usually a woman." And they would be correct. In Pope's time and for many years before, *rape* meant to seize or take, and the seizing or taking of a woman's virtue was just one kind of taking. But as so often happens with words, this one moved from a rather broad meaning to a very specific kind of taking.

And here's a further development. Today we sometimes use the word *rape* in a metaphoric way when we speak of the rape of the land. What we mean when we use *rape* this way is that people are doing violence to the land, which is rather helpless as it is abused. In this context, the word has moved away from meaning a specific act of sexual abuse to a more general kind of abuse. When people use the word *rape* to describe the abuse of the land, they are employing the strongest word they can think of that means "to abuse."

Let me make a further point that seems obvious to me but needs to be made. The word *rape* is not in itself an evil thing, any more than the words *murder, hate, steal, death,* or *Satan* are evil. These words describe evil things. Someone told me recently of a Christian singer who has written a song in which he uses the word *rape* to describe human abuse of the earth. This singer was giving a concert with many Christian school children singing in chorus with him. And one of the songs to be sung by this chorus of junior high students was the song that had the word *rape* in it. But–and here's the reason I'm making this point–some Christian schools pulled their students from the chorus because they didn't want them singing the word *rape*.

I assume these people objected because they think the word is evil. (Incidentally, the other word they objected to is *prostitute*, a word that appears 75 times in the New International Version of the Bible.) Perhaps they don't want their children to know about these words. But surely, if they live in the world of newspapers and television, they *do* know about these words.

It seems to me that the adults who have forbidden their school children to sing in this chorus have either a faulty understanding of language or naive notions about popular culture. After all we live in world where date-rape happens among high school students (even Christian high students), a world where young men and women from Christian families are sometimes sexually active before marriage. That's the reality that the censors in this incident seem to be hiding from.

Rectangle

Recently, while reading a student review of the movie *Saving Private Ryan*, I noticed that the reviewer kept using the word *quadrant* to describe the small band of soldiers who go in search of Private Ryan. Eventually I realized that she meant *squadron*. This sort of confusion of language is not uncommon in student papers, especially if they are based on oral language experiences like movies.

Interestingly, however, her use of the word *quadrant* was not as far off base as I originally thought, for *quadrant* and *squadron* come from the same root. A *squadron* is literally a square, from the Italian *squadrone*, and the word, when used to denote a military group, meant a "square formation of troops." A square is literally a four-sided figure, and the word *quadrant*, meaning a "fourth, a quarter," comes from the same root as *square*.

Since we are talking about four-sided figures, let's look at the word *rectangle*. What the word means literally, and obviously, is "right angle." A rectangle is "a quadrilateral with right angles." The prefix *rect* comes from the Indo-European root meaning "to move in a straight line." Our word *right* (in which the gh used to be pronounced, *recht*) means literally, "straight, that is, not bent or twisted by sin or error." *Correct* means "the right answer." *Reckless* means "without attention to rules or laws." *Direct* suggests "a straight line to a place." To *regulate* is "to impose order on a subject or situation." The Latin word for king, *rex*, comes from this same root, suggesting, I suppose, that the king did what was right and just. Even the word *rectum* carries this idea of straightness, for *rectum* is the shortened form of *rectum intestinum*, and it designates this lower, straight part of the intestine, distinguishing it from the curvaceous remainder of the intestine.

So here we can in one short word make a journey from the highest to the lowest, from *rex* to his *rectum*.

Resurrection

What wonderful pictures words sometimes carry in their histories; yet often we do not know the stories and therefore cannot see the pictures. Take the word *resurrection*. At the root of the word is the Latin word *surgere* meaning "lead up from below." It actually came from two Latin roots, *sub*, meaning "below," and *regere*, meaning "lead." The common English word that we have from that root is, of course, the word *surge*.

Think of the word *surge* for a moment. A surge is a sudden burst. A great wave surges against the rock. We feel a surge of emotion as we see a loved one we have been separated from for a time. We speak of power surges when a sudden burst of electricity blows out the lights or the computer. That surging, that bursting forth that cannot be contained, that's the picture that is the heart of the word *resurrection*. The second syllable of *resurrection* is from the word *surge*.

One of my favorite hymns as a boy was the Easter song "Low in the Grave He Lay." The chorus especially excited me when we sang it: "Up from the grave he arose, With a mighty triumph o'er his foes." The combination of words and music catch the drama of the moment: He surged forth. He did not creep out of the grave, did not peak around timidly and then shyly edge his way between the stone and the crypt. As the second stanza of the song says, "He tore the bars away." In my mind's eye I see him rip that stone out of the way, and there he stands, wild-eyed, wrappings blowing in the breeze. Death's conqueror surges forth.

What a picture, and part of it is in the word *resurrection!*

Now, what about the *re* in *resurrection?* Doesn't that suggest a re-surge, a second surge, a second leading up from below? No, here's the way I would explain that *re*: Christ had been up and on the earth walking about; then he was killed and buried, was put down; then he revived, reappeared, resurged, resurrected.

Seventeenth century poet George Herbert in his poem "The Dawning" captures something of this sudden surge of Christ's resurrection as well as the resurrection that all believers will experience.

The Dawning

Awake sad heart, whom sorrow ever drowns
Take up thine eyes, which feed on earth;
Unfold thy forehead gathered into frowns;
Thy savior comes, and with Him mirth.
    Awake, awake;
And with a thankful heart His comforts take.
But thou dost still lament and pine and cry;
And feel His death, but not His victory.

Arise sad heart; if thou do not withstand,
Christ's resurrection thine may be;
Do not by hanging down break from the hand,
Which as it riseth raiseth thee.
    Arise, arise;
And with His burial-linen dry thine eyes:
Christ left His grave-clothes, that we might, when grief
Draws tears or blood, not want a handkerchief.

David Schelhaas

Salmon

The lake looked as it had on a hundred other cloudy days. My son and I put the boat in the water, the gear in the boat, the motor on the boat, ourselves in with the gear, and off we went. With the wind in our face and our six horsepower Chrysler cruising full throttle, we got, eventually, to the pan fish spot: twenty thick wooden posts, once part of a pier, nearly submerged two hundred yards out from shore.

The water was black, the sky gray. Both cold. The fish weren't biting, which wasn't uncommon, so we sat and talked and fished an empty lake. The day seemed like any other but it wasn't.

For suddenly a miracle happened.

A miracle began to which we were the sole witnesses. We were in a dream—an amazing, beautiful dream. I saw, that day, a dance that I had never seen before, nor ever since, both wonderful and frightening. For suddenly, all around us there were a hundred leaping fish. A thousand. Who could explain it? Huge, speckled, hook-mouthed fish, leaping and splashing on all sides of us. I had never seen fish half that big before and for a moment we were nothing but stunned. Then, for a moment, we fished desperately. But a few casts proved they weren't biting. So we simply watched, amazed, as, in every direction, the fish leaped and fell. We were part of an unfettered celebration of life; it got into our bones, made us shiver and laugh and sing. Our hearts leaped up.

The fish were King Salmon, migrating in leaps and lunges from Lake Michigan, through Muskegon Lake and up the Muskegon River to their origin to spawn. I tell the story because it paints a picture of the salmon as distinct from almost any other fish: a picture of a giant fish leaping.

The name *salmon* actually goes back to a Latin root, *salire*, which means "to leap or jump." Apparently, we were not the first to notice the jubilant characteristic of these leaping fish. Some more scholarly fishermen beat us to it a long time ago and made up the name. Isn't that just like the Romans?

The Latin word *salire* is the root for a number of English words one might not associate with jumping. If you *insult* a person, you figuratively "jump on" him. The original Latin *insulto* was used to describe the way a wild beast might leap upon his prey, or a soldier on his foe. This connotation is retained in our *assail, assault,* and *sally,* that is, "to break out of a defended position suddenly and attack." *Salient* facts are the important ones that "leap" out at you. Something that is *resilient* keeps on leaping up, springing back.

Of course, when I saw the salmon on Muskegon Lake, I did not think about word origins. I saw a wonderful dance of jumping fish and was amazed. Now, upon reflection, I am reminded of a text in Psalm 104 where the poet praises God for the leviathan (see page 60) that He formed to "frolic" in the ocean. And I am reminded that all words have histories and stories; that like the salmon and the leviathan, language leaps and frolics.

Secretary

The word *secretary*, I suspect, brings to most of us the image of a woman typing, taking notes, or answering telephone calls. This is a fairly modern perception, for early in our nation's history secretaries were more likely to be male than female. The word *secretary* also often suggests competence and knowledge. Just last week as I taught a course in our school's graduate program, a number of people came to me with questions about credits and payments and such administrative issues. I did not send them to the director of the Graduate Education program, but to his secretary–because I knew she would be most able to answer their questions and solve their problems. Titles like Secretary of State or Secretary of Education also convey this idea of expertise.

The etymology of *secretary*, however, has nothing to do with either gender or competence. A secretary was, originally, a keeper of secrets. As you might guess, *secretary* and *secret* come from the same source, a word that means "to separate or divide off." So, a secretary was a personal confidante. One early commentator, Heylin, speaks of Moses as one of "God's secretaries," that is, one entrusted with the secrets and commands of God.

The idea of a secretary as a secret-keeper is not common in our time, but wherever people in positions of power and influence are, there are probably secretaries who are privy to secret information. Think of Rose Woods, Nixon's secretary, and the notorious blank spots on the Watergate tapes. She appears to have been such a secret-keeper that she was willing to erase certain key passages on the tapes.

The image we have in our minds of secretaries taking notes is perhaps better captured in a much less frequently used word, *amanuensis*. An amanuensis is an assistant who takes dictation or copies from another manuscript. You see in the word *manuscript* and *manual* and many other words derived from the Latin word for hand, *manu* or *manus*. A manuscript is–or used to be–something written by hand; an amanuensis was the person who did the copying by hand.

I suppose as I sit here typing on my computer, I could claim to be writing by hand, but it is certainly a step removed from the handwriting that involves a pen and paper. Strangely, neither typing nor writing by hand would be called manual labor these days—though both do involve the *manus*, that is, the hand.

In our culture, a secretary is often considered a person of subservience. Yet Nicholas Love in his *Mirror of the Life of Jesus Christ* (1400) writes of Christ taking with him "his three special secretaries, that is to say, Peter, James, and John." One can hardly imagine a higher calling: Christ's secretaries, the keeper of his secrets and commands.

Seethe

The word *seethe* is not used much these days, but when it is used, it means "to be full of anger, ready to explode with anger." Yet until the fourteenth century, *seethe* was the common word used to speak of water boiling. In Chaucer's "Clerk's Tale" we read of a woman who took "Wortes or othere herbes the whiche she shredde and seethe for hir lyuynge." In other words, she shredded carrots and other vegetables and boiled them for her lunch. I dare say none of us uses *seethe* in that way. "Honey, how long have those eggs been seething?"

The shift from *seethe* to *boil* occurred during the thirteenth and fourteenth centuries—after the Norman Invasion—and *seethe* was retained in the language only in its metaphoric sense—"to boil with anger or rage." This change occurs more often in the evolution of language: the original, literal meaning disappears and what remains is a metaphoric meaning only.

Another word for anger, *rage*, works in a somewhat similar way. While it has always meant "fury, madness, frenzy," it derives from the Vulgar Latin *rabia*, from which the word *rabies* also comes. So at one time, *rage* was "the madness or fury that came as a result of being bitten by a rabid animal and contracting rabies." Today, of course, *rage* is simply another word for violent anger.

Ironically, *anger*, the word we most frequently use today to denote fury, rage, or indignation, originally meant something else. As you might guess, *anger* originally meant about the same thing as *anguish*. They came from the same root and meant "distress, grief, affliction." As I have noted in an earlier discussion of the word *narrow*, the origin of these words—*anger*, *anguish*,

95

narrow—is the Indo-European base *angg*, meaning "narrow, squeezed, constricted": The way your chest feels when you are angry.

Seething, rage, anger—all are hard on the body. They are physically unhealthy. They also damage the spirit and destroy relationships. The good word is that the Master who said to the raging, seething, Sea of Galilee, "Peace, be still," says the same thing to us—in our anguish and in our rage.

Shrove

Even though the Tuesday before Ash Wednesday is a religious holy day, Shrove Tuesday, I must confess that I do nothing worshipful or especially commemorative on this holy day. I suspect that's true for most of us.

Shrove Tuesday is the first day of Lent. Down in New Orleans they don't call it Shrove Tuesday, but Fat Tuesday, with Fat suggesting that this Tuesday is the last day to indulge your appetites before the Lenten fast begins. But the word *shrove* suggests something quite different to some religious people.

Shrove is the past tense of *shrive*, and *shrive* means primarily to hear someone's confession and prescribe penances. On Shrove Tuesday a Catholic would make confession and be told what to do as penance. The word *shrive* comes from the Latin word *scribere* meaning "to write," suggesting that the penances may have been written down at one time.

The *Oxford English Dictionary* gives us a picture of Shrove Tuesday or Shrove-tide that seems nearly as festive as Christmas—more like Fat Tuesday than a time of penance and confession. To keep shrove-tide meant to make merry, to go around singing for money. Mothers baked little shrove-cakes for their children who went a-shroving. Florio in 1611 writes of "one that loves to shrove ever and make good cheer." The playwright Thomas Nashe in 1596 writes of sending someone "a couple of hens to shrove with." Again and again, in English life of the sixteenth and seventeenth centuries, *shroving* seems almost to be a synonym for singing and partying and feasting.

The word *shrift* is also a derivative of *shrive*, also meaning "confession." It has survived in our language primarily as a phrase combined with *short*. She was given short shrift, we say, and we usually mean she wasn't given much time or attention or she got, unfairly, a small amount. The phrase originally was used to describe the short amount of time a criminal was given to make his confession before he was executed. Shakespeare writes in *Richard III:* "Make a short Shrift, He longs to see your Head."

But enough. Let me end before you accuse me of giving you "long shrift."

David Schelhaas

Simple

One of the most beautiful contemporary religious songs is "A Simple Song," written by Leonard Bernstein and based on Psalm 96, "I will sing a new song to the Lord." My youngest daughter, who loves to sing and loves this Bernstein song, has talked of singing it in church some time. I told her that would be a great idea, but there was just one problem: The song begins, "Sing God a simple song, Make it up as you go along, Sing like you like to sing, God loves a simple thing, For God is the simplest of all." Now what does that mean, I asked her. It sounds almost blasphemous to say that God is the "simplest of all."

About then my son chimed in with "I wouldn't worry about it too much. After all *simple* is used to describe God in one of our church's confessions, The Belgic Confession. Right at the beginning, the first or second sentence." Sure enough there it was: "We all believe in our hearts and confess with our mouths that there is a single and simple spiritual being whom we call God."

Well, that information prompted me to make a trip to the *Oxford English Dictionary* where I learned the following: *simple* comes from two roots, the first syllable from a word meaning "same or single"; the second syllable from a root that means "fold or ply." So that literally the word means "same fold" or "single fold." The central idea then is "oneness."

This idea of singleness or oneness is probably at the heart of the Belgic Confession's use of the word. But *simple* must mean more than that, for it is used in conjunction with single, "a single and simple spiritual being." Why would the Belgic Confession repeat the idea of simplicity?

Perhaps it intends something else as well. Already in the thirteenth century, *simple* was used to mean "free from duplicity, innocent and harmless, open, honest, straightforward." John Wycliffe translates Luke 11:34 as follows: "The light of the body is the eye, If your eye is simple, your whole body is full of light." Here the meaning seems to be "open, honest, straightforward, trustworthy." No deviousness is shrouded in the simple eye.

Here's another example of that meaning: A standard modern translation of Zechariah 9:9 describes the coming King as "meek and lowly and riding upon an ass." Miles Coverdale, in his translation of 1535, describes the Christ-King as "lowly and simple." Here the word suggests "humility, freedom from pride and ostentation"–another standard meaning of *simple* four hundred years ago. These meanings are all very positive, easily applied to God. He is one, absolutely trustworthy, incapable of sinful pride.

The negative meanings of *simple* also go back a long way. Already in 1340 *simple* could mean "deficient in knowledge or learning," and by 1600 it also was used to mean "foolish or stupid." This meaning was probably advanced by the singing and reciting of the nursery rhyme "Simple Simon."

In any case, for a long time in the history of the word, positive and negative connotations existed side by side. Today, unfortunately, the word's intent is most often negative, carrying the baggage of Simple Simon. Even our use of *simple* to mean "uncomplicated," though close in meaning to the original idea of oneness or singleness, is not entirely positive in connotation. But in the Belgic Confession and Bernstein's wonderful song, *simple* is clearly a positive word that draws on its earliest meanings: single-fold, trustworthy, free from pride. "We believe in a single and simple being whom we call God." It's that simple.

Snoop

An enterprising employee in an office area near my office has a small cache of candy and other goodies that he sells. The little business depends upon the honor system; you put your fifty cents in a plastic container and choose your sweet. The sign at the top says "Snoops R Us," and as I read it, I wonder if people who are not of Dutch background would understand, for *snoepen* is a Dutch word for sweets, candy especially. They might, for when I check the *OED*, I discover that the first definition of *snoop* is "to appropriate and consume dainties in a clandestine manner."

Apparently there's something sneaky about eating those sweets. For it is from that usage that the more common American use of *snoop* has developed: a snoop is "someone who goes about in a sly or prying manner." He pokes his nose in where it does not really belong–but in a sneaky way. Sometimes, in fact, the snoop is an eavesdropper.

And what is an eavesdropper? The original meaning of *eaves* is "going over the edge." It comes from the German, and our English word *over* probably comes from the same word as *eaves*. The area between the house and the place where the water dripped from the roof was called the eavesdrop or eavesdrip. Thus someone standing in this area with his or her ear to the door or window, listening in, is called an eavesdropper. The act of listening is called eavesdropping. (I suppose people who are frequently caught by eavesdroppers saying and doing silly things might logically be called eavesdrips, but, as far as I know, they are not.)

These snoopy eavesdroppers, when they run to tell others the juicy stories they have heard, become gossips. The word *gossip* comes from two words, god and sibling (meaning "relative"). Literally, then, gossip meant "relative in God or spiritual relative," and it was used to refer to a godmother or godfather, people chosen at baptism to be the spiritual mentors for children. As late as 1711 this meaning was used. For example, Hearne writes, "I was fully designed to come and stand gossip in person to Dr. Hudson's child."

But by the fourteenth century, it had also come to mean "close friend." In the nineteenth century, the great Romantic poet John Keats in his "Eve of St. Agnes" writes, "Ah, Gossip, dear, we're safe enough. Come in this chair and sit."

And by the sixteenth century it also meant "one who indulges in idle talk, a bearer of tales, often false ones." John Dryden uses the word this way in 1687 when he writes of "the common chat of gossips when they meet."

As you can see, all three meanings existed side by side for several hundred years. But that is not true for *gossip* today. Only the third one has survived: "As a noun designating an idle talker, as a noun designating the idle talk itself, and as the verb designating the act of talking idly."

What an immense semantic shift–from "spiritual relative" to "one who prattles loosely, often doing irreparable damage with half truths or outright falsehoods." Yet how marvelously creative humans are as they take words for candy (snoop), the drip edge of a roof (eavesdrop), and godfather/godmother (gossip), and make of them all words for sly, nasty people.

Spigot

When I was a boy I worked in my father's grocery store, an old fashioned sort of place where in the summer, during canning season, we sold vinegar from a fifty-gallon wooden barrel. People brought in their gallon jugs, and we placed them under the spigot, opened it, and filled the jug. But before we could do that, after the vinegar barrel arrived from the fruit and vegetable wholesaler, we had to knock the bung, that is, the wooden stopper, out of the barrel and jam the wooden spigot into the bunghole.

The word *bung* comes from the Dutch and before that from the Latin *puncta*, "to pierce," from which we also get a word such as *puncture*. Thus it sounds as if the bung was first of all the hole; eventually, however, it came to be the wooden or cork stopper in the mouth of a cask or barrel.

The word *spigot*, which is still frequently used today, comes from the Old Italian *spigorare*, which meant "to tap a cask or barrel." It is either the plug used to stop up the hole in the cask—and could thus be a synonym for *bung*—or more commonly today, the faucet that was inserted into the hole of the cask or the tap that you turn on to get water. (At my house the outside faucets are much more likely to be called *spigots* than the inside ones. I don't know if that's typical or not.) *Spigot* actually goes back to the Latin *spiculum*, which means "a point or a spike." The thing that was pounded into the barrel, whether it was a faucet or cork, was spike-shaped, narrower on one end than the other.

I just used the words *faucet* and *tap*. The word *tap* comes from an old, old word that means a cylindrical stick, the same word that gives us *tap-root*. This word *tap*, which today, like *spigot*, we use to designate a faucet, was originally a stopper inserted into a keg.

Finally, we should look at the word *faucet*. And it presents me with some difficulties. My *Webster's New World Dictionary* tells me that *faucet* comes from a Latin root that means "false" or "to falsify." Here's how this root relates to the device we call a faucet. To make a breech in something—as you do when you make a hole in a barrel—is to falsify it in the old sense of the word, for you make it less than whole, weakened at some point.

But when I turn to my *Oxford English Dictionary*, which is supposed to be the final word on words, I see nothing about falseness. Rather, I am told the word *faucet* is of unknown etymology. But the meaning is clear: "A peg or spigot to stop the vent-hole in a cask; a vent-peg." So again we see that as with *spigot*, the early meaning of *faucet* was "the peg or stopper." Only later did it come to mean "a valve." The *Oxford English Dictionary* also gives an interesting distinction between spigot and faucet. Both words refer to an old form of tap "consisting of a straight wooden tube, one end of which is tapering to be driven into a hole in the barrel, while the other end is closed by a peg or screw. The peg or screw when loosened allows the liquor to flow out through a hole in the underside of the tube. Properly, the *spigot* seems to have been the tube and the *faucet* the peg or screw." Today that distinction seems to have been lost and *faucet* and *spigot* are used as synonyms.

Spigot does seem to be the older of the two words, for in Wycliffe's 1388 translation of Job 32:19, we read, "Lo! My wombe is must with out spigot ether a ventyng that brekith newe vessels." The 1430 edition substitutes *faucet* for *spigot*. In case you are wondering what this verse means, the King James Version says, "Behold, my belly is as wine which hath no vent; it is ready to burst like new bottles." Elihu is speaking. Elihu has been listening to Job's three friends, and he is so angry at what they have said, he is ready to explode; he's like a wineskin or barrel with no vent, no spigot, to let out his feelings of anger toward Job's unfair friends. In the very next verse he says, "I will speak that I may be refreshed: I will open my lips and answer." So you see, his mouth becomes the spigot and his words are the liquor or vinegar that give him relief. Words have the capacity to relieve us when we are ready to explode. That's a good thing—most of the time.

Soffit

Every craft, every area of work, contains words that seem strange to the layperson but absolutely ordinary and everyday to the person who works in that occupation. I have just finished reading Cormac McCarthy's great western novel, *The Crossing*, which is filled with cowboy language: What is a *dally*? A *twitchrope*? *Pommel* and *hackamore* I know, but they are also part of that horsey, cowboy vocabulary. I suppose this specialized vocabulary could be called jargon—but it is not jargon in the bad sense, that is, the use of language to confuse or overwhelm the hearer with large, strange sounding words. Rather this specialized vocabulary is language that enables speakers to communicate precisely. Writers like to use the precise word, and consequently they are interested in these kinds of words when they write on a particular subject. A writer does not want to say *doohickey* or *whatchamacallit* or *thingamajig*. She wants to say cotter key or slip-joint pliers or garlic press.

For many summers I was a painter and because of that I was amused recently to read an e-mail inviting me to a church work-bee to paint, among other things, the *muttons* of the windows. Actually the writer should have said *mullions*. But perhaps she did not know what she was typing when she sent the e-mail—for *mullion* is not a household word. Or perhaps she is from the Northeast, where if I can trust what I heard on a recent production of *This Old House*, *mutton* is a regional variation of *mullion*.

What is a *mullion*, you ask? "A slender dividing bar between panes of glass in a window." It comes from the Old French for *middle* or *median*; mullions divide windows right down the middle.

Another window word is the word *sash*. To explain that word, let me ask a question: What do windows and cars have in common, besides glass? The answer: they both have a chassis. You see, the word *sash* is really just a form of the French word *chassis*, which means "frame." And so, today, glaziers

101

and painters and carpenters speak of the window sash, its frame, its chassis. *Sash* usually refers to a sliding window frame, in contrast to a fixed window, which is called a *casement*. The poet William Cowper writes in 1781, "The southern sash admits too strong a light./ You rise and drop the curtain, now it's night."

The window sash should not be confused with the sash one wears around the waist or over the shoulder. This sash comes from the Arabic word for turban. Writing in 1599, Fitch says a "great store of cloth is made there of cotton and Shashes for the Moores."

A third word that I learned as a painter, though I'm sure most people know this word simply because it is a part of their house, is the word *soffit*. A *soffit* is the horizontal underside of an eve. Painters aren't crazy about soffits because scraping and painting them is often a miserable job. But the origin of the word is interesting. It comes from the same word as *suffix*, an ending attached to a word to change its meaning or function in a sentence. The Latin *suffixus* means "to fasten on beneath." The soffit is made up of boards, sometimes ornamental, that are fastened to the underside of the roof. Since I have saved the word *soffit* for my last paragraph, it functions as a sort of suffix or soffit for this little piece on painters' jargon.

Sostenuto

Anyone who has taken piano lessons or sung in a choir has seen them—those funny looking words above the treble clef, words like *vivace*, *dolce*, *allegro*, *adagio*, *scherzo*, *fortissimo*, *poco pio moso*, *sostenuto*. Many of us when we took piano lessons wondered why composers couldn't just "say it in plain English," but musicians, like most specialists, like their specialized and universal language.

Recently I read a poem that had, as an English word, the word *sostenuto*. I had to look it up, of course, and in so doing I discovered that *sostenuto* comes from the same source as our word *sustain*, and that *sostenuto* means "played at a slower, but sustained tempo, with each note held for its full value." *Sustain* comes from two Latin words: *sus*, which is a form of *sub* and means "under," and *tenere*, which means "stretched" or "held." From this root we get such words as *thin* (like a sheet of metal or skin stretched over bones); *tenuous* (so thin or fine as to be insubstantial or flimsy); *tense* (like a stretched rubber band or nerves–ready to break). So something sustained is stretched out underneath, like a low organ note that continues while the melody unravels in the treble.

The poem that contained *sostenuto* still needs some explanation, however. Richard Wilbur begins his poem "For C." describing love relationships that don't last but have dramatic partings. Then, in the conclusion of the poem the speaker speaks of "long love" and seems to addresses his spouse of many years:

> Still, there's a certain scope in that long love
> Which constant spirits are the keepers of
>
> And which, though taken to be tame and staid,
> Is a wild sostenuto of the heart....

A long marriage has the s*ostenuto* quality of being steady, sustained over a long time. Yet by speaking of a "wild" sostenuto, Wilbur creates a combination of opposites, an oxymoron. How can a *sostenuto*, a slow, sustained tempo, be wild? I don't know if it can in a musical composition, but it seems to me a perfect description of a long, good marriage: Sustained, steady over months and years and decades, like the steady beating of the heart, yet also punctuated with wild heart beats, wild joy, wild romance, wild grief, and even anger. A long, good marriage is indeed a "wild sostenuto of the heart."

Sound

Etymologists and others who study the histories of word origins sometimes disagree about how a word came to mean what it does or even what roots it has derived from. This is not surprising, since the changes in what words mean and how they are pronounced are not usually made according to some plan. They just happen, and they usually happen so gradually that nobody lives long enough to hang around and watch the change occur. Historians have to make educated guesses sometimes as to why a word that used to mean "uncomplicated" now means "stupid."

Dr. Barry Sanders is an English professor and cultural historian. In his book *A is for Ox* he says that the word *sound* meaning "healthy" came from the practice of doctors–still used today–of thumping people on the chest as a technique to assist them in the diagnosis of their health. He compares it to the practice of sounding the depths of the ocean to determine how deep the water is. Well, that's a wonderful story, and when I read it I was pleased to learn where the phrase "being of sound body" came from. The word *sound* meaning "healthy" or "well-made" or "undamaged" comes from this thumping that doctors do. Unfortunately, Barry Sanders is wrong.

After checking a number of sources, I think I can assert that this meaning of *sound* comes from the same word that the German *Gesundheit* comes from. This word, as most of us know, means "health" and is often said after someone sneezes. The Dutch *gezond* is also from the same West Germanic source. This use of *sound* meaning of "healthy" or "undamaged" or "reliable" is used frequently–especially in the translations of Paul's letters to Timothy where we see references to sound doctrine at least four times.

The use of the word *sound* to measure the depths of the ocean comes from a different source all together–the Latin combination of *sub*, meaning "beneath," and *unda*, meaning "waves." The letter "B" in *Subundare* gradually disappeared and *sound* remained.

Sound has another meaning associated with water, but it also is from a completely different source. The word *sound* that means a "channel" or "strait," as in Puget Sound, comes from a word that at an earlier time meant "to swim." It comes from the Old English *sund.*

Finally, I must mention the most obvious meaning of *sound*, "noise" as a noun or "to make a noise" as a verb. This word comes from the Latin *sonus* and means simply "sound." Other words we use from that same root are *dissonant, resonant, sonata, sonnet,* and *sonorous.*

This meaning is not only the most familiar to us, it was also the most frequently used meaning in the *King James Bible*. Psalm 19 tells us that the heavens declare (sound forth) the glory of God and that the God-declaring words of the skies speak to the whole world so that all may hear of God. Paul picks up on this in Romans 10:18 when he says, "Their sound [the words uttered by creation] went into all the earth and their words unto the ends of the world."

Spill

A great summer treat for me, after the busyness of the school year, is to read a murder mystery by P. D. James. James, an Englishwoman, writes novels that are always intricately plotted and have strong moral themes. A member of the Church of England and an astute observer of character, James recognizes the innate depravity of humans but also the power of faith to sustain and give life.

She is also a fine stylist with a broad knowledge of the English language, so it is not surprising that I would run into a word used in a way that was new to me. Our word today is *spill*, which, in *A Taste for Death*, James uses as a noun to designate a piece of paper used to carry fire from one source to another: A piece of paper is ignited in the fireplace and then used to light a candle on the mantle. The paper is called a *spill*.

I check my dictionary, and sure enough, under *spill*, noun, this definition appears: "a splinter, thin roll of paper, etc., set on fire and used to light a pipe, candle, etc." Now I must find out, first, the source of this noun and second, whether it is connected to our verb *spill*, meaning "to allow or cause, accidentally or unintentionally, liquid to flow over from a receptacle or container."

The noun *spill* meaning "a splinter or roll of paper used to carry fire" is not, I discover, related to the verb *spill*. The origins of the noun *spill* are not clear. It may come from *spile*, a word of Germanic origin meaning "a splinter or wooden peg or even a spigot." But it might also come from the word that gives us *spin* and *spool*. Quite likely all of these words—*spigot*, *spool*, *spin*, *spill*—come from the same root.

The verb *spill* originally meant "to take a life, to kill." In fact, from 1200 to 1600 this was the common meaning of *spill*. It is not difficult to see how the meaning of *spill* moved from "kill" to our present meaning, "causing liquid to flow out of a container." The most obvious way to kill someone is to injure him in such a way that the blood spills out of his body. Thus we see in the language the old pattern we have talked about before, the meaning of a word moving gradually from something specific to something more general. With *spill*, the meaning moves from killing by shedding human blood to causing any kind of liquid to escape from or flow out of its container.

An old English hymn, "Now Synge We," which goes back to 1529, has these lines spoken from the point of view of Christ:

> Thus was I spylt,
> Man, for thy gylte,
> And not for Myne.

It is comforting to know that even though words change their meanings gradually over time, God's plan of redemption is unchangeable: Christ was killed because of human guilt, and not for anything he had done. That truth remains, yesterday, today, and forever.

Starboard

The other day, after dining with friends, our host read from the gospel of John, the twenty-first chapter where Jesus says to his fishing disciples: "Cast your net on the starboard side of the ship." The word *starboard* surprised me. The only translation it appears in, as far as I know, is the Revised English Bible. I wasn't able to find an explanation of why this particular translation used *starboard* rather than *right* (perhaps the original Greek uses a nautical term rather than a simple direction word, or perhaps it is a very English word), but I *was* able to discover how *starboard* came to mean "right."

Starboard is a corruption of *steerboard*. Early Germanic peoples propelled and steered their boats by means of a paddle or rudder on the right side of the boat. Thus the steerboard side, that is, starboard side, was the right side. Gradually, the idea of a steering board disappeared, and the location of that board took over as the dominant meaning.

We have a number of compound words that mean almost literally what they meant several hundred years ago, but their pronunciations—like that of steerboard/starboard—have changed, sometimes masking their obvious meaning. Breakfast, for example, is simply the time when we break the fast that a night of sleep has imposed on us. And so we eat. Breakfast.

And cupboard (which we pronounce *cubboard*) is quite simply a cup board, that is, a board on which to store one's cup when not using it. Actually, it was probably closer to what we would call a sideboard today. (My wife tells me that I am one of the few people in America who still uses the word *sideboard*, so, perhaps *counter* would be a better word choice here.) Eventually, of course, as people acquired more and more dishes, they did not have room to store them on the counter (sideboard), and so cabinets had to be made for them. But we still called them cupboards, or rather, *cubboards*.

I will conclude with two *eye* words. You know, of course, that a daisy is really a day's eye, the yellow orb at the center of the daisy resembling the eye of the day, the sun. But perhaps you did not know that window means "wind's eye." The Viking word for window was *vindauga* and it meant wind-eye. I suspect that since they did not have glass and lived in the Northern climes, the Viking's, when they threw open the shutters, opened the eyes of the house and allowed the wind to enter it.

Window, daisy, cupboard, breakfast, starboard: With a slight twist of the tongue they become *wind-eye, day's-eye, cup-board, break-fast, steer-board*, and their first meaning becomes immediately apparent.

Subtlety

Here's a good word: *subtle*. *Subtlety* is a desirable quality most of the time. In contrast, *sneaky* strikes me as a bad word, an undesirable quality. A sneak cannot be trusted. Sneaky behavior is deplorable. Both *subtle* and *sneak* may suggest something that is not quite open, not obvious, but *sneaky* has a negative connotation and *subtle* a positive. (I realize that exceptions to these designations can be found. The serpent of Genesis 3:1, for example, is described in the King James Version as "subtle.")

Subtle carries the connotation of being fine, delicate, mysterious, not immediately obvious. *Subtlety* suggests nuance. So much of our life is nuanced. Right now it is spring, and the trees and fields are all green. I suppose that as a child, all I saw was one color, green. But I have learned to look at things more carefully and now see many different shades of green, subtle differences that give beauty and texture to the landscape.

The word *subtle* comes from two Latin words that mean "under (sub) the tile, that is, the textile." It refers to the weaver's shuttle passing under the web-threads of the loom, making a cloth that is a mixture of color and design, finely textured, not immediately apparent. Another definition of *sub tile* says it a bit differently: "beneath the lengthwise threads in a loom." The picture this definition gives is much the same: Background is provided for the main design.

As I have said, so much of what we delight in comes from subtlety. A joke, even the most elementary kind, depends on a subtle use of language. Ole comes home and sees his barn is on fire. He runs into the house and calls the fire department. "Fellas," he says, "This is Ole. You've got to come right away. My barn is on fire." "Okay, Ole," they say, "How do we get to your place?" "Well, why don't you take that big red truck you have in the garage there?" Ole says. The joke depends on our recognizing a subtle use of language–How do we get there?–that Ole, the immigrant, does not recognize.

Why can Sister Wendy see so much more than I can when she looks at a painting? She recognizes the subtleties of color, shape, arrangement, line, subtleties that I have not learned to see. Why can a mechanic listen to my car engine and tell me that the timing is off? He hears something that I don't, a subtle variation from what should be heard.

Good poetry is almost always subtle–finely textured. A word connects or contrasts with a word used three lines earlier to make some sparks fly if you have the eye to see their glimmer or an ear to hear their buzz.

So many problems develop in politics and religion, it seems to me, because people think in black and white. And black and white do not allow for subtlety, for nuance, for the shades of color that the Creator has woven not only into the landscape but into the entire fabric of our lives–even the world of ideas. These shades, these subtleties, make life interesting, but also complex.

In Book VIII of Milton's *Paradise Lost*, the angel Raphael warns the pre-fall Adam from investigating too deeply "Things remote from use, obscure and subtle." He is talking especially about knowledge of the planets in deep space. I don't agree with Milton here, but I suppose it is possible that some things are too subtle, too mysterious for human exploration.

But not language. A word can have as many shades of meaning as the spring landscape has shades of green.

Teetotaler

The other day a couple of friends asked me to explain the word *teetotal* or *teetotaler*. The word had come up, they said, as they were enjoying a beer with their pizza. A *teetotaler*, as most of us know, is someone who totally abstains from alcoholic beverages. My first inclination was to say that the word came from England and probably stood for someone who drank only tea. That, however, is a pretty dumb answer since the *tee* of *teetotal* is spelled *t-e-e*, not *t-e-a*.

My second thought was of a quote from C. S. Lewis in *Mere Christianity* where Lewis is discussing the cardinal virtue of temperance. He writes, "It is a mistake to think that Christians ought all to be teetotalers. Mohammedanism, not Christianity, is the teetotal religion." Lewis then goes on to note that it may be the duty of particular Christians in a particular time to abstain from alcohol, but that teetotalism is not a cardinal virtue, required of all Christians.

Well, that makes sense but takes us no closer to an explanation of the word. Where did this strange word come from? At least three stories exist.

The first story and the most credible, I think, is that the word was an emphatic form of the word *totally*. Here the first letter of *totally* is added to the front of the word for emphasis: "The game was not just awesome and it was not just totally awesome. It was T-totally awesome." The thing to note about this story is that it has nothing to do with drinking unless one uses *T-totally* as an adverb modifying *abstinent*.

A second story is that the *Tee* in *teetotalism* is a shortened form of the word *temperance*. In other words, t-totalism is temperance-totalism. It suggests complete avoidance of all intoxicating beverages. This leads us to our third story.

Richard Turner, from Preston, England, is said to have coined the word in 1833 advocating total abstinence from intoxicating liquors of all kinds, in contrast to the practice of some early temperance reformers who abstained from "ardent spirits" (what we would call hard liquor) only. Even on his gravestone, Turner is credited with being the author the word *tee-total*.

Wherever the truth lies, we know that today a teetotaler abstains from the drinking of any alcoholic beverages.

Let me conclude by making a comment about the word *temperance*. Temperance was traditionally one of the cardinal virtues, but it did not refer only to drink. Rather, it was applied to all pleasures–moderation in all things, as St. Paul says. Another writer calls for "self restraint in the indulgence of all natural affection or appetency." Eating, working, shopping, playing, making love, even loving our children can be excessive and intemperate. When they are, we sin.

Temperance–from the Latin *temperare* which means "measured, regulated, mixed"–would be a good word to restore to its full meaning, and teachers and pastors could be instrumental in doing that by using it in its broader sense. Alas, it will not happen because I want it to or even if a decree mandating such a change comes down from the Supreme Court. Words will be what they will be.

Tenor

When I noticed that the word *tenor* came from a word that meant "stretched out" or "held," it made perfect sense to me. Years of singing in choirs has given me a mental picture of tenors who could not quite reach the high notes they were required to sing and therefore bent back their heads and stretched out their necks in an effort to reach the notes. Of course, I thought, tenor equals stretched out.

But that is not really an accurate image of the source of the musical term *tenor*. This idea of being held or stretched out referred to the voice that held the melody, and back in the fourteenth century that voice was the tenor voice. Gradually, we began to call the range of that voice *tenor*. Today we call men who sing in that range *tenors*.

Before the word *tenor* was applied to music, it meant (and still means today), "a continuous course, that which is held to." We say "the tenor of his argument was this and that," and we mean the main idea that he held to as he made his point.

Many, many words in our language come from that *ten* prefix. One is *tennis*. Before I discuss the meanings of that word, allow me a diversion. The game we know as tennis was preceded by something called *real tennis* or *royal tennis*. It was a game played on a rectangle divided by a net and enclosed by four walls off of which the ball might be played. (Both *real* and *royal* derive from the word *realm*. Perhaps the four walls were seen as a kind of realm.) Real tennis sounds a bit like racquetball, but only the highest classes played it. As late as 1954 someone wrote, "The games of real [royal] tennis and piquet are still marks of the upper class."

Now to the reason tennis is called *tennis*. Sometimes, today, when we play tennis, we shout "service" to our opponent before we serve the ball so that he or she can be ready to receive the ball. Well, six or seven hundred years ago, the server would shout "Tennis," that is, "Hold" as a way of telling his opponent to get ready to receive the ball. Here again we see the idea of holding stiff or tensing up.

Other words from that root are these: A *tent* is a "stretched skin spread over a frame." A *tenant* is "a holder, one who holds the land." A *tenet* is "a belief, that is, what you hold to."

And *tender* has two quite different meanings. *Tender*, the one that means "to offer," as in "He tendered his resignation" also carries the idea of holding out or stretching out. On American paper money is the sentence: "This note is legal tender for all debts, public and private." In that sentence *tender* is a noun, but one that suggests the same meaning as the verb used in the phrase "tendered his resignation." The five dollar bill is offered, is held out as payment for services or goods. It is legal tender.

And then there is that other, beautiful word, *tender*. Does a sweeter, warmer word exist in our language? When we say the word, we think of a mother caring for her small baby, of our father God embracing us, his prodigal children, as we come back to his house, our home. What does this *tender* have to do with being stretched or holding to? Think of it the way you might think of the word *tendril*, a word we use to describe a delicate, tender shoot of flower or grass. *Tender* carries in it the idea of stretching out gently, delicately.

In the song of Moses recorded in Deuteronomy 32, we have this wonderful image of tenderness: "My doctrine shall drop as the rain, my speech shall distil as the dew, as the small rain upon tender herb, and as the showers upon the grass." Tenderness is not a thunderstorm, but "distilled dew" and "small rain."

Tidy

"What's the connection between the tides of the ocean, the *tide* of the phrase 'tide you over,' and the word *tidy* as 'she kept a tidy house?'" I was asked recently. Like Mark Twain in *Life on the Mississippi*, I was gratified to be able to answer promptly. I said I didn't know. But since then I have learned that they all mean essentially the same thing.

They all come from the word that gave us the word *time*, and hence all have a meaning connected to the idea of time. When we use the old saying "Time and tide wait for no man," we are really being redundant. Or almost so. Actually the *ti* of *tide* comes from the word that gives us time, and the last half of the word come from the word that means "to cut up." *Tide*, then, is "time cut up, time portioned out." *Tide* was used to describe the rise and fall of the ocean because it designated the fixed time of high tide and low tide. Note that I said the fixed time of high and low tide.

The verb *tide* in "tide you over" really means "last for a time," so again you can sense the time notion in the word. Phases like Christmastide and noontide simply mean Christmastime and noontime.

Tidy is a bit more complicated. At one time it meant "timely or seasonal." From the thirteenth century right up to the late 1800s, *tidy* also meant "fair, well-favored, bonny, fat, plump." A bit of farming wisdom from the 1500s goes as follows: "If weather be faire and tidie thy graine, Make speedily carrege, For feare of a raine." At the same time *tidy* came to mean "excellent, or satisfactory" as in the phrase "a tidy fortune." From that idea of excellent or satisfactory emerged the modern meaning of "neat and clean."

The word *tidings* seems to come from a different source, a word meaning "to happen or occur." Tidings are, of course, news of something that happens, but we don't use the word much anymore. The *King James Bible* has the angels bringing "good tidings of great joy." But more recent translations use the word "news."

One of Henry Wadsworth Longfellow's best poems is "The Tide Rises, the Tide Falls." If you read it aloud and listen to yourself carefully, you can hear the beat of the tide as it measures out time in the rhythm of the poem.

The tide rises, the tide falls,
The twilight darkens, the curlew calls;
Along the sea-sands damp and brown
The traveller hastens toward the town,
  And the tide rises, the tide falls.

Darkness settles on roofs and walls,
But the sea, the sea in the darkness calls;
The little waves, with their soft white hands,
Efface the footprints in the sands,
  And the tide rises, the tide falls.

The morning breaks; the steeds in their stalls
Stamp and neigh, as the hostler calls;
The day returns, but nevermore
Returns the traveller to the shore,
  And the tide rises, the tide falls.

Tuition

I've been paying Christian school tuition–kindergarten through college–for more than 25 years and have participated in tuition drives and tuition studies, so perhaps I can be excused for thinking I knew what the word *tuition* meant. Recently, however, I found out that I have a very limited understanding of what *tuition* means. Reading the latest novel by British detective writer P. D. James, I noticed that she describes as a tuition session a student going to study with his professor's supervision. Tuition? I thought she must have made a mistake; surely she meant to write tutorial session. So I loaded up the on-line *Oxford English Dictionary* to check out the word *tuition* and discovered she had used *tuition* in a perfectly acceptable way.

In fact, it is not until 1867 that *tuition* is used to describe money paid for educational services, and even then it is as a hyphenated word, *tuition-fee*. So our use of *tuition* to mean "money" is really a shortening of the longer *tuition-fee*, where *fee* means "money" and *tuition* means "an educational service rendered." Like *(omni)bus* and *auto(mobile)*, *tuition* is a clipped word. But in keeping just half of the word, we have given to that half *(tuition)* the meaning of the other half, *fee*.

The word *tuition* comes from the Latin *tuitio* meaning "to look to or to look after." From the twelfth century to the nineteenth century, the most frequent use of *tuition* seems to be this idea of looking after, protecting, caring for. We read phrases like "pray for the tuition of the church," and "the protection and tuition of orphans." J. Hooker, in his *Life of Sir P. Carew*, says, "I commit your lordeship to the tuission of the almightie."

The word *tutor*, which comes from the same Latin root and which we use almost exclusively in an educational context, also carries, in its earlier usage, the broader idea of a guardian, one who has custody of a ward. In his translation of Galatians 4:2, Wycliffe uses the word *tutor* where the modern New International Version uses *guardian*.

So far, I have established that *tuition* once meant "protection" and *tutor*, "guardian." As far as I know, both can still be used that way, but gradually, both came to have a meaning associated with education. Even while *tutor* meant guardian, it was also used to mean "a mentor," a personal teacher. And *tuition* was used to mean "training or education" as early as the sixteenth century.

Now if your intuition is telling you that the word *intuition* is also from this Latin root meaning "to look to" or "to look after," then your intuition is working well. But *intuition* has made a bit of a journey from its original usage to its contemporary use. Today we use *intuition* to mean a kind of looking or sight that comes not by hard, logical thinking, but by a sudden almost visionary revelation. We speak of "a woman's intuition" as a kind of knowing that is almost instinctive.

A writer in 1497 speaks of people having a perpetual "intuition of ... infinite joy," that is, a looking through to, an envisioning of, infinite joy. The English preacher Jeremy Hooker uses *intuition* in a somewhat more literal sense when he says that the disciples of Christ "must not onley abstain from unlawful concubinate, but from the impurer intuition of another man's wife." In other words, Hooker says, "Don't take a second wife and don't even look at another man's wife and envision her as your sexual partner."

P. D. James uses *tuition* legitimately when she uses it to describe an educational session. Perhaps you could instruct your child to ask for her tuition as she walks into her classroom next September. "I've come for my tuition," she might say to her teacher, that is, "I've come to be looked after, to be mentored, to be instructed."

Umbilical

Have you ever taken umbrage at someone or at something someone said? An unkind remark perhaps? *Umbrage*. It's not the most common word in the language, but then it's not unfamiliar to most of us. We kind of know what it means: "offense or resentment." It comes from the Latin word *umbra*, which means "shadow." The phrase "to take umbrage" follows a sort of metaphorical extension from shadow to suspicion and from suspicion to resentment.

If I told you that we have other words from that same Latin word for shadow, you would probably think of *umbrella* and you would be right. An *umbrella* is really a little shadow–from the Italian *ombrella*.

Two other words familiar to us come from combining the Latin *sub* meaning "under" and *umbra: sombrero* and *somber*. Put on a sombrero and you are under a shadow; put on a sad face, a somber face, and you are emotionally under a shadow.

And then there is *penumbra*, the partly lighted area surrounding the complete shadow, the *umbra*, of a body such as the moon during an eclipse.

Now as my index finger glides down the dictionary page, the finger stops at *umbo*, a word I've never heard of. It is defined as "the knob at the center of a shield." We don't use shields much, and that is probably why we don't know the word. But we all do know a part of our body described by a related word; in fact, all of our lives depended on it at one time. From the same root as *umbo* comes *umbilicus*. Nowadays, we use the adjective *umbilical* as a synonym for a life-giving cord of some kind, an astronaut's line attaching him to the space capsule or a river that waters a plain. But first of all, *umbilicus* refers to that knob at the center of our bodies to which our umbilical cord was once attached, our navel.

Of course most of us don't call it a navel or an umbilicus. We have a better designation for it. I can't think of single body part that is more aptly named than the "belly button." I wonder if any other language quite so accurately and alliteratively captures the essence of the funny little swirl at the center of our bodies, "belly button." It's not only an accurate visual representation, but it also suggests the silliness of this little blip on our tummies: If we could just unbutton it we could step out of our skin. Or if we pushed it, somehow our engines might start up. I suspect no one knows who invented the phrase "belly button," but he was most certainly a poet.

Proverbs 3:8 tells us that the fear of the Lord "shall be health to thy navel, and marrow to thy bones." I wonder if any of the modern paraphrasers of scripture have rendered *navel* as "belly button." I hope so.

David Schelhaas

Vegetables

It's June and my garden is full of growing things: beans, peas, cabbage, onions, carrots, tomatoes, and much, much more. Right now, things are rather tame, though I am already harvesting peas, lettuce, and radishes. But late July and August are the really exciting times for a gardener. Then the harvest starts in earnest: golden potatoes; red cabbages; watermelons so ripe, red, and juicy that they crack when you cut them; glossy, deep purple eggplant, so gorgeous it should simply be set on the table as a centerpiece to look at. And tomatoes–huge pink Brandywines; sweet, sweet Black Crims, a Russian variety that never gets red, but gets black on top when it is ripe; and all of the other interestingly named red ones: Beefsteaks and Big Boys and Early Girls, and so on.

Some say the tomato is a fruit; I call it a vegetable. I'm not really concerned about who is correct, but I am interested in the word *vegetable*.

Vegetable comes from a Latin word that means "healthy, lively, vigorous, fresh." In fact, *vigor* comes from the same source as *vegetable*.

For many years, centuries, in fact, *vegetable* meant any growing thing, any plant. Most of us have played that old guessing game, "Twenty Questions" which uses the three categories "Animal, Vegetable, or Mineral." Any vegetation was called a vegetable. This meaning of *vegetable* existed from the mid-1500s to the mid-1800s. In 1884 Oliver Wendell Holmes says of two trees that they are "both pleasant vegetables."

By the late 1700s, however, our present use of *vegetable* as a certain kind of food plant was beginning. Thus we see the word narrow from a broad term meaning any green-growing plant to a term that designates edible foods that come from plants.

Go back with me now to the original Latin meaning: "healthy, lively, vigorous." These sound like good words to describe the qualities of the vegetables we eat. However, common slang usage has given us another meaning for *vegetable* that is exactly the opposite of lively and vigorous. "He's nothing but a vegetable," we say sadly of a person with a severe brain injury who seems to have no life or vigor. George Bernard Shaw writes in *Back to Methuselah*, "What use is this thousand years life to you, you old vegetable?" The implication is that anybody a thousand years old is not likely to have much vigor or to move about much.

I suppose this slang meaning has developed because unlike animals, *vegetables* pretty much stay in one place until they are harvested. Hence also our phrase "couch potato" rather than "couch monkey" or "couch sloth."

115

But I much prefer the original and still operative meaning of *vegetable*. What marvelous gifts from the hand of the Creator. They themselves are full of life and health, and they bring life, health, and vigor to us when we eat them. We remember the story of Daniel and his three friends who ate "nothing but vegetables" and were "better nourished than any of the young men who ate the royal food." Perhaps there's a nutrition lesson there.

Virtue

> Whan that Aprille with hise shoures soote
> The drogte of March hath perced to the roote
> And bathed euery veyne in swich licour
> Of which vertue engendred is the flour.

These are the first four lines of the "Prologue" to Chaucer's *Canterbury Tales*, written in the English of his time—the mid 1300s. We call that English, Middle English, to distinguish it from Old English which was the English spoken up until 1066 and which sounds like a completely foreign language to us today. Middle English, Chaucer's English, was the English spoken and written between 1066 and 1500; Modern English is the English spoken since 1500.

As a high school English teacher, I sometimes required my seniors to memorize and recite in Middle English the first 18 lines of Chaucer's "Prologue." One of my favorite memories from that time is hearing and seeing a group of senior soccer players huddled together before the game and reciting this prologue in Middle English at the top of their voices.

If you are unable to make complete sense out of Chaucer's Middle English, here's a modern translation:

> When in April the sweet showers fall
> And pierce the drought of March to the root, and all
> The veins are bathed in liquor of such power
> As brings about the engendering of the flower.

I began with these lines of poetry to remind you that the words of the English language change not only in meaning but also in spelling and pronunciation. *Aprille* becomes *April*; *drogte* becomes *drought*; *roote* becomes *root*. But I also chose this quatrain because I have always been somewhat puzzled by Chaucer's use of *vertue* in the fourth line—"Of which vertue engendred is the flour." What does virtue have to do with the coming alive of flowers?

116

When we use the word *virtue* today, we usually mean good and right actions and thoughts—the opposite of vice. But the origin of the word is the French *vir* meaning "man," and the literal meaning of the word is "manliness, valour and worth." The same root is used in our word *virile*, which means "manly strength or vigor."

Now, if we take that idea of vigor or vitality, we come close to the meaning Chaucer intends in the *Canterbury Tales*. As early as the 1200s, *virtue* meant "the power inherent in a supernatural person," that is, in God. And so when Chaucer writes "of which vertue engendred," he is speaking of the "licour's" life-giving qualities within the flower, but, beyond that, of God, the ultimate source of that vitality and power.

Eventually, the *virtue* came to mean not only the power inherent in God but also the God-like qualities that the people of God exhibit. In the ancient church, the three theological virtues were faith, hope, and charity. The cardinal virtues—those recognized by all civilized people, not just Christians—were prudence, temperance, justice, and fortitude. And so we see the pilgrimage that *virtue* makes, starting out as "manliness, vigor, vitality," moving to the idea of "God as the source of vitality and strength," and ending up as a word that encompasses "all the God-like qualities that people can display."

What a good word!

Wax

Most of us know the old hymn, "Jesus Shall Reign Where'er the Sun," which ends with the couplet "his kingdom stretch from shore to shore,/till moons shall wax and wane no more." Those verbs, *wax* and *wane*, are both nearly obsolete today.

Wane means "to decrease in size, to dwindle." Literally it means "lacking or wanting"; in fact, it comes from the same verb as *want*. We may still hear *wane* in a phrase like the "waning hours of the twentieth century," but for most of us, the use of *wane* is on the wane.

Wax, as used in the hymn, is also out of use. Again, we may use a phrase like "waxing eloquent," but it is really a sort of archaic rhetorical flourish. In the King James translation of the Bible, however, the verb *wax* is used often: According to the book of Exodus, God's anger often "waxes hot" against the Israelites. In Matthew 24, which records the Olivet discourse, Jesus says that in the last days, "the love of many shall wax cold." Clearly

117

wax here means "to grow or increase." In the first quote, heat increases, in the second cold increases.

The English verb *wax* comes from the Indo-European base *woks-*, and although it is not much used in our language, related words from that base are still frequently used in other languages.

The noun *wax* is still very much in use in our language; however, it is not related etymologically to the verb. Those of us over forty remember yellow paste wax that was polished on the linoleum floors to give them a shine after they had been mopped. Nowadays that kind of wax–the yellow paste wax–is rarely used, but many other kinds of waxes are used–car waxes, furniture waxes, paraffin. We also speak of earwax, that yellow sticky substance that we get out of our ears with a Q-tip or our pinky.

Wax originally meant, specifically, bee's wax. It comes from a word, *wakhsam*, that meant "woven," since beeswax was found in a comb woven by the bees.

Wax is rarely a yellow paste today, and it certainly is not woven. Though not yellow, paraffin (the white wax that is often used to seal the jar when making jam) is probably the closest thing to the old wax. But the word that referred to a yellow, sticky substance still hangs around, usually meaning "a substance that gives luster when it is applied to something and polished."

On the other hand, the use of the verb *wax*, meaning "to grow," is waning. Why does one word adjust to changes and continue to be used while another gradually disappears? I don't have a clue.

Yahoo

Most of us know the word *yahoo* as an exclamation of extreme delight, "Yahoo," or as the name of a search engine on the web. An effective way of finding information on almost anything is to go to www.yahoo.com on the web.

Yahoo is a word coined by Jonathan Swift in his great classic, *Gulliver's Travels*. In that novel, Yahoos are a race of brutish, degraded creatures that look like humans and have all the vices of humans. Swift, you remember, was a satirist who reserved his most savage criticism for humans–their terrible selfishness, cruelty, and indulgence in the sins of the flesh. In *Gulliver's Travels*, the Yahoos are the servants of a much more civilized race of creatures called the Houyhnhnms, creatures who look like horses but have human reasoning powers and human virtues. The word *Houyhnhnm* was coined to sound like a whinny; in other words, it is an onomatopoetic word.

We can sense the sting of Swift's satire when we realize that the horse-like creatures are far more civilized than the man-like creatures. Because of the brutish and depraved nature of the Yahoos, the word *Yahoo* has been used for several hundred years to describe people who are coarse, uneducated, anti-intellectual, and crudely materialistic. For example, in the *Western Canadian Dictionary and Phrase Book* of 1912, *yahoo* is defined as a "lout from the back country, an ignoramus, a know-nothing."

Sometimes, it seems to me that we are very rapidly entering into the age of yahooism. A recent article in the *Chronicle of Higher Education*, "The Obsolescence of the American Intellectual," suggests that as well. We live in a visceral age, an age when people are much more likely to value the emotional, the intuitive, or the instinctive rather than the intellectual. It is possible that in an earlier age the emphasis on intellect and reason was overvalued. For centuries reason was looked upon as the most God-like quality in humans, the quality that most carried the imprint of God's image. However, the present trend away from the valuing of the intellectual and towards a valuing of the visceral and the sensual appetites, especially as seen in American popular culture, is a trend toward yahooism. Swift's Yahoos are deplorable creatures, and the fact that many today have not heard of him is perhaps one small indication of contemporary culture's march toward yahooism.

The search engine Yahoo! is probably named after the exclamation one makes when one finds the information he has been looking for. That's a wonderful kind of Yahoo. I hope that as you have read these brief discussions of words, you have been moved to exclaim "Yahoo!" in amazement and wonder at the English language, in the same way that you might exclaim "Yahoo!" or "Hallelujah!" when you consider the heavens on a starry night. The Psalmist declares in Psalm 19 that the heavens declare the glory of God, and a clear night will confirm that for almost anyone with an eye to see. But other things give testimony to the presence of God as well, and one of these is certainly language. Consider the history of the English language, its staying power, its remarkable flexibility, its sheer volume, its ability to withstand onslaughts from other tongues as well as from native speakers. Consider its logic, its whimsicality. Consider how it can be used to arouse a nation to go to war and cause a maiden to fall in love. How concrete it is, yet ephemeral; how personal it can be, yet universal. Consider the meandering journey some words have taken to their present meaning while others mean exactly what they did 500 years ago.

Language in its complexity, versatility, vitality, and whimsicality speaks to me of a creator God, a God who used language to speak the world into existence and sent his Word made flesh to rescue the world from its self-inflicted despair. "Hallelujah! Yahoo!"

Acknowledgements

My thanks to Kim Rylaarsdam, Jeri Schelhaas, Bob DeSmith, Sally Jongsma, and Heidi Karges for reading and editing these words at various stages along the way. Thanks also to John Kok for steering this project through to completion. And thanks to the many friends and colleagues who over the years have said, "You ought to do this word, or what do you know about that word?" And finally, I'm grateful to Dennis De Waard for giving me time on KDCR radio to do the weekly spot "What's the Good Word."

Printed in the United States
135109LV00004B/4/A